*Choral Music
of the World*

Choral Music of the World

PERCY M. YOUNG

Illustrated with photographs and music examples

Abelard-Schuman

LONDON · NEW YORK · TORONTO

By the same author
World Conductors
World Composers
Keyboard Musicians of the World

© Copyright Percy M. Young 1969
L.C.C.C. Number 68–18091
Standard Book Number 200.71608.5

LONDON
Abelard-Schuman
Limited
8 King Street
WC2

NEW YORK
Abelard-Schuman
Limited
6 West 57 Street

TORONTO
Abelard-Schuman
Canada Limited
1680 Midland Avenue
Scarborough

Printed Offset Litho in Great Britain by
Cox & Wyman Ltd, London, Fakenham and Reading

Contents

Illustrations

To Renée,
late of the Cantata Singers,
New York

Preface

IN one way or another, most of us get involved in choral music, sometimes willingly, sometimes unwillingly. I have often known people to have been persuaded to join a choir in order to put some tenors where there were none before, or otherwise to "make up the numbers". A surprising number of such conscripts have become devoted choral society members. It is true that among these there have been some without any special musical talent; but they have proved useful in many ways—by looking after the music, or marking the attendance registers, by collecting subscriptions, or (when desired) making tea or coffee or (in the case of the strong) moving the piano. Choral music, in short, is the most social form of musical activity. I hope that it may long remain so.

But there is more to it than this. Or, rather, we must explore other meanings of the word "social" and see how it includes many aspects of society. In so far as music has any connection with what goes on in the world at large, choral music shows this connection most clearly. It has, through the ages, been associated with religious, political, national and international movements. The intent in this book is to show these connections and, in so doing, to increase the interest of the reader in this branch of music. Perhaps the reader who is also a singer, will find his or her pleasure in singing enhanced. The point is made later on, especially by Thomas Morley, the madrigalist, that this particular form of pleasure is further heightened when the singer is at least a competent sight reader.

Many people come to their first practical experience of music through membership of a choir. I am not alone in believing that this is the best kind of basic experience for a full understanding of music. Through singing with other people, one becomes caught up with the texture of music, and in this way comes to appreciate both how and why music is made. One is not looking in from the outside, but looking out from the inside.

To some extent this book is written from the inside, for, in addition to accounts of choral organization there are also more or less detailed references to the varying techniques of choral composition. To explain these, there are numerous, annotated, music examples. It is hoped that the reader will take the hint and try to sing them (so far as possible) and thus improve his ability to read music. The modern G and F clefs are used, but on p. 50 clefs not now in general use are shown. Modern practice in using only two clefs in choral music may be con-venient in some ways, but when a composer could drop his C clef on any line he was able to avoid that bugbear of the present system—the leger line. Moreover, we still have to cheat. The tenor part is written with the same clef as the soprano (or treble)—the G clef; but below it we must put 8 to show that the notes sound an octave lower.

When the reader has digested this and sung the melodic lines of the examples, he should try to put them together and play them on the piano. While doing so, however, he should carefully watch the movement of the individual parts and also try to imagine the proper vocal tones. From here, he will go on to a study of as many works as are recorded as possible (see the select list of recordings on p. 201). At the same time, if he is a choir member, he will be studying the works chosen for him to sing with interest and care.

In addition to music examples, there are numerous illustra-tions. These are to be regarded as a part of the story and not merely as decorations. They have been chosen so that the reader may feel himself in the company of singers at different times and in different places. He should, however, be diffident about anticipating membership of any angelic choir. I have heard singers who sound like angels; but beyond that it would be unwise to go.

Foreign words to be found in some of the music examples are given in translation on p. 199.

The music example on p. 193 is quoted by permission of Boosey and Hawkes Ltd.

P.M.Y.

Randolph-Macon Club of New York
February 10, 1969

I

What is Choral Music?

IN olden times, especially in Europe, choral music was held to be a superior form of art, for it was the one above all others in which angels were presumed to be perfect. It became, therefore, the aim of every human singer—who was brought up to look forward to the possibility of a heavenly career sooner or later—to qualify himself for membership of the angelic choir. The story of the Nativity of Christ, at which the hymn "Glory to God in the highest" was supposed to have been sung for the first time, and the paintings, sculptures, and carvings and music, that have sprung from it, have all inspired the idea that group singing of religious songs has a particular merit. A beautiful painting by the Renaissance artist, Piero della Francesca (1416–92), of Florence, is shown on p. 16. References to music concerning the Nativity are to be found on pp. 132, 175, and 180.

The idea that ritual song has its own special virtue is much older than Christianity, but in this book we shall not look back beyond the earliest forms of choral singing in the Western church.

The term "group", in connection with singing, at the present time has a particular meaning. It refers to one kind of singing, by performers who have their own characteristics, which would seem to take us a long way away from the image described in the first paragraph. Curiously, however, the two kinds of groups

are not as far away from each other as might appear. Any present idea of "heaven" is probably far distant from the conventional one of the medieval churchgoer. But the effect of popular group singing of today is to stimulate many to a belief that they either have arrived, or will arrive, at a state of unique pleasure.

Choirs of angels (represented by the robed choristers of the church) held out hopes of escape from an imperfect world. Groups of "Beatles", and their successors and imitators, also hold out to many somewhat similar hopes.

This has nothing to do with the essential character or quality of particular kinds of music. It is merely that the human voice is a powerful agent, forever working on the emotions. It is the medium by which we express the widest range of thought and feeling. Thought goes into words, feeling into sounds that often are less definite than words. The gap between thought and feeling is bridged by song. The beginning of singing was in the sound patterns that can be produced by the voice. But these patterns when applied to words bring out, as it were, the emotional feeling lying behind the words. Song is a point at which reason and imagination meet. To many people this meeting seems to be a mystery. This accounts for the fact that singing has at all times, and in all places, played an important part in religious development.

We may take the supposedly angelic text, "Glory to God in the highest". This may or may not make sense when spoken. When sung by a choir, it seems to many—and always has seemed—to make a great deal of sense. The words of a contemporary popular song by themselves are frequently nonsense, but when they are set to music they appear to achieve some kind of purpose. The listener may say, and believe, that "the message gets across".

This book is about choral singing. It may be wondered why, up to now, it seems to be assumed that choral singing (singing by a group of people) is superior to solo singing (singing by one person). In fact there is no such assumption. There is no superiority of artistic merit in the one kind of singing or the other. There is, however, a difference of function. The solo singer is an individual. In some cases, as in that of the bard or the minstrel, he may appear as a mouthpiece for a community. A company of singers, however, being a group, and a cross section of society, is more easily recognizable as representative of a community as a whole, and the larger group often identifies itself with the smaller group. Something of the same thing occurs in other spheres. In that of sport, for instance, a nation sees itself in a national team.

In the widest sense of the word, choral music has been long associated with religion—with ideals which belong basically to a spiritual context. This association, worked on by religious leaders for thousands of years, has tended to narrow down the general approach. If you join a church or chapel choir you will naturally sing settings of special texts. If you join a choir not connected with a religious body—whether in or out of school— you will almost certainly find yourself singing some of the same material. Otherwise, you will expect to go through a repertoire of standard "oratorios". Some of this will be excellent music; some of it will, by any standards, be great music; some of it may be very bad. Some of the best music ever composed is choral music; so also is some of the worst. The last category has often been justified on the grounds of moral uplift. To understand this, one only needs to look at some of the poor music that is to be found in most popular hymnbooks.

All of this is a measure of the importance of choral music. It occupies a special place in the experience and development of society, and thus has always attracted attention from the leaders of society, and from teachers. Each community has swung into action on the stimulus of choral singing. Therefore, from time to time, we all stand up and sing a national anthem, a hymn, a party song, a school song. . . .

From this general kind of involvement we develop many of

our responses to the whole art of music. Because in certain situations music, with words, takes on meaning, we tend to interpret music without words—instrumental music—into similar and derivative shades of meaning. This is cheerful; that is not. So we begin to examine what we think music is about. Within the field of Western music we may well be right in thinking in this way, since, for at least 1,500 years music-with-words was considered to be more important than music-without-words. The influence has remained strong, and it is difficult to escape the conclusion that any musical work, because it has "something to say", is more than a mere abstract pattern of sounds.

One further point, so far hinted at, should be made clear. Choral music is the one branch of musical performance in which the not especially gifted individual may take part with a maximum of pleasure to himself and a minimum of inconvenience to his neighbours. So far as technique is concerned, choral singing ranges widely, from the incomparable excellence of certain bodies—to be named later—to the modest standards to be discovered in any small community in almost any country. Choral singing is an art, but it is also a social activity, and important in both respects.

The fine choir shows what singers, collectively, can do. The inferior choir (however much its members may derive satisfaction from its efforts) usually shows what singers cannot do, or —musically speaking—should not do. This brings us to the limitations of choral music.

All musical activity is subject to limitations. A violinist cannot play chords which the pianist can, nor can he play deep-sounding notes such as belong to the double bass. Yet it is precisely because there are limits on what may be done that music, in the end, makes sense. What is impossible focuses attention on what *is* possible. What is possible constitutes character and encourages quality.

Of all musical instruments the voice is at once the most simple and the most complicated, the most familiar and the most

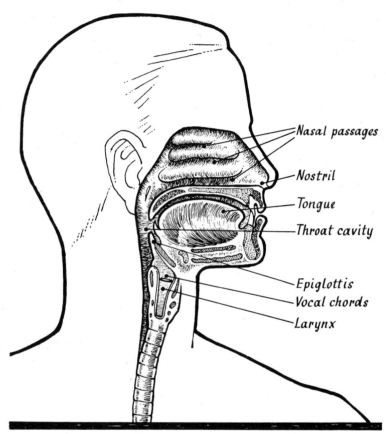

Nasal passages

Nostril

Tongue

Throat cavity

Epiglottis
Vocal chords
Larynx

The LARYNX

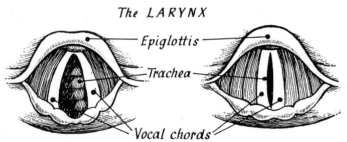

Epiglottis

Trachea

Vocal chords

During respiration

During speech

Organs of speech

remote. The voice is a wind instrument. Air is taken into the lungs to form a wind supply, which is controlled by an apparatus of muscles. Air compressed in the lungs is driven at will towards the two tiny strips of cartilage contained within the "Adam's apple", known as the vocal cords. These vocal cords, when moved by the escaping wind flow, vibrate in exactly the same way as reeds in a woodwind instrument. The vibrations thus created are amplified, by cavities in chest, mouth, and head. They are then picked up by a listener and recognized as sound.

Sounds produced in this way are distinguished by character, by pitch and by quality. So far as pitch is concerned this is determined by increase or decrease of the tension of the vocal cords. It is almost miraculous that each one of us is capable, unconsciously, of adjusting the vocal cords so that sounds of particular pitch are produced. In speech, we vary pitch according to the type of message which we wish to convey, and according to the conventions contained in the speech habits of the group of which we are members. In singing, we adjust pitch to the demands of a pattern of sounds (a melody) already existing. Some achieve this adjustment more or less easily; others require a good deal of practice. A few miss out on this capacity. They are usually, but not necessarily quite accurately, described as tone deaf. Tone deafness, however, is a convenient term if it reminds us that, in singing, the ear is in partnership with the voice.

We quickly find out that the range of a voice is limited. We cannot produce sounds of every pitch, only of some, and in musical terms they lie approximately within the limits of an octave and a half.

Sounds begin to make some sort of sense because of their pitch. They are equally significant by reason of quality. Here it may be said that no two voices are exactly alike. It is possible for one violin to be replaced by another without the listener noticing any difference. With two voices, regardless of the number of similarities of tone quality there may be, this is not possible. The factors that make for distinctions in vocal quality are many and complex. It is sufficient to say that just as the material from which instruments are made affects their tone, so physical structure affects the quality of the voice. There are, of course, certain broad distinctions to be borne in mind. The voice of a child is quite different from that of an adult; that of a woman is different from that of a man. There are differences of singing tone—especially noticeable in choral singing—between nations. Some of these differences are due to the nature of language. Italian, for instance, which is heavily marked by the purity of vowels, makes for one kind of tone, whereas German makes for another. One notices also differences of intensity in choral tone. What is known as "continental" tone is frequently thought to be "harder" than English or American tone, although it is considered ideal by some for certain kinds of music. In England and America there may be heard choirs which specially cultivate this tone for old music.

Leaving aside the matter of quality we may again consider that of pitch. The voice of a child produces high sounds. So, in general, does that of a woman. Men's voices, on the other hand, cover a range of deeper sounds.

These facts of nature have a great influence on the character of music. Because some kinds of high sounds are produced by children music composed for children to sing may be suggestive of certain qualities credited *to* children. In modern times, Gustav Mahler and Benjamin Britten have made frequent use of the characteristic quality of children's voices in order to suggest a feeling of innocence. The high sounds of women's voices are also used evocatively in order to indicate feminine qualities, so that the "flower maidens", for example, in Wagner's music drama *Parsifal*, sing music that is easily accepted as being as alluring in its own right as are the maidens in theirs. If one wishes, on the other hand, to suggest manly courage then it is sensible to wrap it up in the particular tones of men's voices, as—to take an obvious case—in the "Soldiers' Chorus" in Gounod's *Faust*.

These are naturally the simple facts of the situation. But they are fundamental. For on these simple facts the structure of choral music has been built.

It is not enough to divide voices into high and low, for within these groupings there are subdivisions. Some women have voices of a different working register from others. One woman may find (Ex. 1) comfortable and (Ex. 2) uncomfortable to sing.

EX. 1   EX. 2   EX. 3   EX. 4

Another may find the reverse to be the case. The former (with practice) will conveniently cover the range (Ex. 3), the latter (Ex. 4). The first singer will be described as a *soprano*, the second as a *contralto*. The higher notes of the one and the lower notes of the other will be found to be the most effective. A third type of female voice may be discovered, lying between the two already mentioned. This is described as *mezzo-soprano*.

The broad distinction of high and low in respect to men's voices gives the definition *tenor* and *bass*, with sounds lying somewhere about an octave lower than the soprano and contralto voices.

Corresponding to the mezzo-soprano is the *baritone* type of voice—higher than the true bass and lower than the true tenor.

Children's voices, which are somewhat more variable than those of adults, cover (or can be made to cover) the soprano or contralto registers. At the age of puberty a boy's voice changes or "breaks", to use the popular term, and acquires tenor or bass quality. Unfortunately, there is no guarantee that a pleasant boy-soprano tone changes into an equally pleasant tenor or bass. Johann Sebastian Bach was distinguished as a boy chorister. After his voice had broken he was not acceptable to his choirmaster as a singer. He was, however, found to be useful in other ways—as copyist, accompanist and instrumentalist.

Since a voice is capable of producing sounds of different pitch, within the limitations already described, it is clear that a singer may shape a melodic line without too much difficulty. The melodic line may be said to become melody when the sounds present an orderly pattern to the listener. In the first place, melodies grew out of the pitch differences within speech. Rise and fall of pitch, and length and intensity of sounds, were an extension of language; and because words and melody were inseparable, music that was sung—as has already been suggested—occupied a border territory between two forms of expression. At some periods, composers have tended to stay on the musical side of this territory, so that there are many songs of which the words are little more than convenient pegs on which to hang music. At other periods, composers have preferred to emphasize verbal values (see pp. 100 and 196). At all times, however, the majority of composers have agreed that the first duty is to invent a convincing melody. If this were not the case, of course, singers would have something to say in the matter!

A vocal melody is essentially a simple form of expression. In order to achieve satisfactory practical results a composer is well advised to remember that a singer—especially one who is unaccompanied by an instrument—is happiest when he or she can (a) remember a melody, (b) find a natural and reasonable relationship between the sounds that constitute the melody, (c) feel a meaningful connection between melody and words, and (d) discover satisfaction in presenting the said melody to an audience. In short, a singer's melody should be singable.

There are two kinds of vocal melody. One is for the solo singer, the other for a group of singers. It stands to reason that the first may be more ambitious than the second—unless the group comprises only singers who are qualified to be termed soloists in their own right. In this connection it may be observed that in the seventeenth century many German composers wrote music for voices for two groups, the one much more highly trained than the other. The trained group was given more or less complicated melodies (though well within the limits of practicability), the less efficient group more or less simple melodies (see pp. 44–5).

Melody is a word that is very important in regard to song. It is quite possible to have instrumental music that, in the accepted sense, is melodyless. Much music of the present time may be, and often is, so described, and there is no reason to suppose that it is either better or worse for the lack of melody. That is a matter of style, taste and judgement. But unmelodic song is inclined to sound uncomfortable, if for no other reason than that the unfortunate singer appears not to know where he or she is going. It should, however, be made clear that forms of melody are not static, but change from period to period—even from composer to composer.

From what has already been said, it is clear that sung melodies can lie in different regions. The soprano melody is higher than the contralto melody. This is higher than the tenor melody, which in turn is higher than the bass. When we listen to a group of singers we are immediately aware of the existence of separate vocal parts, each functioning within its own area, and each with its own distinctive tone quality.

Choral music, then, is a combination of tone qualities and of sounds of different pitch, arrived at through the extension of melodic principles. As we listen to a choir, however, we notice that different aspects of what we hear captures our attention. If we listen to the nearest church choir singing a familiar hymn we recognize that the important melody is given out by the top part, the soprano. Beneath that melody, more often than not, the other voices provide supporting sounds that have no important melodic function. We say (and feel) that the supporting sounds "harmonize" with the melody. One stage further in the vocabulary of the theory of music we describe the collective sounds at any particular moment as "chords". The way in which chords follow each other is called "harmony". Harmony is one side of music, and in the first place it was largely developed through choral music.

On the other hand, there is no reason why each voice (or each group of voices) in an ensemble should not enjoy its own independent melody. Once upon a time, at family parties in Germany and Austria, it was quite the thing to indulge in such an exercise. One group of people would sing one tune, another group a second tune, yet another a third tune—and so on, all at the same time. The tunes were usually folk songs. The result was called a "quodlibet", which means roughly, "everyone to his own fancy". Every year the members of the family of Josef Haydn used to meet at a little town in Austria called Bruck. Singing "quodlibets" was a regular feature of their parties.

Now in a "quodlibet" of this kind, the listener (if there is one) is interested by the interplay of melodic lines. Sometimes, and in some places, he was also interested in the way in which the words were somewhat naughtily altered. Whether he knew it or not, his attention was riveted to the "counterpoint", that is the simultaneous presentation of vigorous and independent melodic patterns.

At this point, it is clear that we are dealing with a subject of some complexity. There is melody—a complex of pitch and of rhythm—which in respect to vocal music is made more involved by reason of its relationship to language. There is harmony, a series of relationships between sounds as they occur at single points in time. There is counterpoint, the relationship between lines of melody presented to the listener during a particular period of time. But melody, harmony and counterpoint do not really exist independently of one another. A musical work is a whole, and the listener, while ready to appreciate and sometimes to isolate one element or another for his private satisfaction, is advised to remember that this sense of totality is of the greatest importance.

The gap between the point at which song begins and the point at which the listener hears a great choral work—such as

J. S. Bach's *St. Matthew Passion*—is a large one. This gap is filled by a whole series of technical advances, social changes, agreements and disagreements that are, in themselves, a record not only of musical but also human development. It is strange, but true, that only in modern times—that is within the last 200 years—have women been allowed to take part in public in choral music. It is strange, but true, that for several hundred years composers were given instructions as to what kinds of scales and what kinds of rhythms they should use, and what kinds of melodies they should compose. It is equally strange, but equally true, that it took something like a thousand years (of European history) to develop a system whereby choral music could more or less effectively be learned from written notation. Lastly, it should be pointed out that what is considered as choral music—music to be sung by a lot of people—as we know it, is of very recent date. All of this is tied up with changing attitudes not only towards music but also towards people.

Before we go further, we should look around and see what kinds of choral music there are within our own environment and experience.

There are church and chapel choirs. For practical reasons, since these are allotted a relatively restricted space in a building, they are fairly small. Those choirs which belong to the older church traditions, more often than not comprise only boys and men. This is because the ancient rules only allowed male singers. During this century the rules have been relaxed somewhat to allow girls and women into church choirs, because boys (and men) are sometimes harder to find than used to be the case. The quality of a boys–men choir is distinctive, and music often gains in clarity of outline what it otherwise misses in emotional feeling. Some choirs of this kind are world-famous—such as the choir of St. Stephen's Cathedral in Vienna (of which the boys alone are known as the "Vienna Boys' Choir"), of King's College, Cambridge, England, and of St. Thomas's Church, Leipzig, Germany. In America the choirs of St. John's Cathedral

and of Trinity Church, in New York, represent the same tradition, even though the foundations are much more recent. The great European choirs have seven or eight hundred years of tradition behind them, which, together with their associations, has helped to give them a public image. The choristers of King's College, Cambridge of today are shown at rehearsal in the illustration above.

If you go to hear a large-scale choral concert—perhaps a performance of Mendelssohn's *Elijah*—you will still see several hundred singers stationed behind a large orchestra. These will be amateur singers, for whom a choral society is a congenial means of making friendly contacts and also of indulging their liking for music. Apart from anything else, what will be specially noticeable will be the volume of tone and the quality of the tone. So far as the volume is concerned (provided that the choir is efficient), the loud singing will be impressive; but the soft singing may be even more impressive. A fine example of the use of this particular kind of loud-soft contrast is in the chorus, "Behold, God the Lord passed by!" in *Elijah*. In comparison with the tone quality of a boys–men choir, that of a large mixed-voice chorus, however, will inevitably seem more impersonal, and, in a way, less "pure".

The large choral society came into being in the late eighteenth century and reached a peak of popularity in the nineteenth century. Many large and celebrated choral societies still function—if for no other reason than to sing some of the master-pieces (like *Elijah*) which were designed on this scale. But the twentieth century has seen a reaction against this kind of choir.

There are now many small groups, either with one or two voices to a part, or comprising not more than, say, thirty or forty singers. The reduction of numbers leads to higher efficiency and to greater flexibility, since the smaller the group the more highly trained the individual members must be. Moreover, the great majority of choral works were thought of and first per-formed by small bodies of singers. Madrigals, for example, were for a single voice to a part. The cantatas and other choral works of J. S. Bach were for a body of between twenty and forty singers. Handel's oratorios—of which *Messiah* is still at the top of the list of popularity rating for this kind of music—were also designed for forty chorus singers, at most. The diversity of small choirs is exemplified by the current lists of recordings and by radio performances. To some extent the mechanical reproduction of music has had something to do with the growing pop-ularity of the small group, partly because groups have been formed specially for recording or radio purposes, and partly because it is made clear to singers in general what a wealth of music there is for small choirs.

Because choral singing is a social function, its character is dependent to some extent on social conditions. Particular social groups have developed their own choirs. Apart from the churches, other bodies which have affected the history of choral

[29]

music include schools, universities, women's organizations, trades unions, and sometimes municipalities. In the history of English choral music the tavern of former times exercised strong influence, for it was there, with their beer before them, that singers first began to enjoy singing secular music.

It is generally recognized that in the broad sense some nations have a stronger choral tradition than others. In Britain the Welsh are especially noted for their zeal for choral music. In Hungary and Czechoslovakia choral tradition was an important factor in the development of a truly national music. German choirs were always numerous and often famous. That these facts stand out is due as much to the influences that shaped the various musical institutions concerned as to the intrinsic qualities of the institutions themselves.

The facts of choral musical life lie very close to what goes on in everyday life. It is the *living* quality of choral music which is its immediate attraction. Choral music comes from people and not from instruments (even though it may be, and often is, accompanied by instruments), and so produces a particular emotional effect. When Josef Haydn was in London in 1791–2 he heard a choir of 6,000 children—the "charity Children"—in St. Paul's Cathedral. He was, literally, moved to tears. This brings us back to the fundamental point that the human voice is, perhaps, the instrument that most quickly stirs the emotions.

A singer, however, does not prove very effective if he or she relies only on "feeling". It is necessary to have a technique. The chorus singer is not exempt from acquiring a technique even though well-meaning people sometimes encourage the inexperienced or inefficient to join choirs "to make up the number", as they say. The two things that matter are to be able to sing in tune, and to be able to read at sight. These are the minimal requirements. Having acquired this two-fold ability, the young singer will be assured of a warm welcome whenever he comes to offer his services. To join a choir is, perhaps, the best means of entry into the world of music.

[30]

2

Foundations

OF the choirs which are famous today—some of which have already been mentioned on pp. 27 and 28—a number grew out of church foundations. If we listen to a public performance or to a recording by one of these choirs, it is likely that we shall find ourselves in areas of music with which we are unfamiliar. Working backwards from contemporary composers, like Stravinsky and Britten, through the Romantic, Classical, and Baroque periods, we arrive at a large body of music for voices belonging to the era of the Renaissance.

During this period, which was also that of the Reformation, we encounter a great development in the field of choral music. Much of it, we will notice, is sung without accompaniment. Unaccompanied choral music is often described as *a cappella* (literally, for the chapel).

At the time when the present Basilica of St. Peter, in Rome, was nearing completion, when the doctrines of John Calvin and Martin Luther were beginning to take effect in many parts of Europe, there was an abundance of music for voices. There were large and important groups of composers of such music in Italy, France, the Netherlands, Spain, Britain, Austria, Germany and other smaller countries in central Europe. The music composed comprised hymns, masses, motets, antiphons, anthems, chorales, on the one hand, and "songs" (in parts) and madrigals, on the other. Within the field of church music, some was for Catholic and other for Protestant use. This was a period of great change. It was the point at which one set of traditions reached a climax, and another set of traditions began to take shape.

Choral music was of great importance during the Renaissance period, because it was the form of music in which composers could best show their skills. It had been practised under the protection of the church, which was why it advanced faster than other kinds of music. The climax of this development is apparent to us in the works of Palestrina, Lassus, Victoria, Byrd —and (literally) hundreds of other composers of the sixteenth and seventeenth centuries.

But, because of the present availability of recordings and the enterprise of many scholars and contemporary groups of singers, we can push back behind this era, to listen to music of the fifteenth and fourteenth centuries. By a curious paradox, the further back we go towards the centre of medieval musical thought, that music, in some respects, sounds, not more "ancient", but more "modern". This is because a number of modern composers have been inspired by some of the principles of style of the Middle Ages. In medieval music the mathematical element in note values and rhythmic patterns was regarded as specially important, and this factor has influenced the most recent music for voices of, for example, Stravinsky. The sonorities, and the sense of mystery particularly bound up with medieval religious dramatic music have inspired Britten.

There is one constant factor in all church music from the twelfth century back to the very start of the Western choral tradition: the importance of one particular set of melodies. The whole of the first era of choral music is dominated by the songs of the liturgy of the Church of Rome. These were composed in the scales known as "modes" and were free in rhythm, that is to say, the singers made the notes conform to the rhythmic nature of the words. This type of music is called "plainsong".

The development of choral music depended on the attitudes of successive generations of singers (and composers) to these

[32]

songs, and on the attitudes to the singers of their employers. Liturgical music, conveniently summarized as "Gregorian music"—since it was codified in the time and under the direction of Pope Gregory "the Great" (ruled 590–604)—appears at first as unison song (that is as a single line of melody). Somewhere about the twelfth to thirteenth centuries Gregorian songs were to be heard arranged for two and three voices. A hundred years later, such songs were the basis of four, five, or six-part compositions. They remained fundamental to most compositions until the time of the Reformation, but with a gradually diminishing status.

During the nineteenth century, plainsong melodies began to be introduced into non-church music, for the value of their dramatic associations. An important work of the early twentieth century which makes splendid dramatic use of two plainsong melodies is the *Hymn of Jesus*, by Gustav Holst (see p. 189).

Christianity was imposed on Europe (as later elsewhere) partly by force, partly by persuasion. In so far as persuasion was employed this was frequently of an indirect kind. That is to say, the arts—especially of architecture, painting, sculpture and music—were used (as we would now say) as a means of advertisement. Music was particularly effective, for singable tunes were also the means whereby particular word-ideas could be conveyed. Ideas presented in this way get under the skin. Logic is defeated by the powerful action of the emotions on personality, so that all of us are persuaded to a particular attitude when we hear certain types of word-music formation. Familiar examples of such persuasive music are the Christmas music of Handel's *Messiah* and the "Crucifixus" music of Bach's *Mass in B minor*.

The basic songs of the Church were relatively simple. That this was the case was due to an early, puritanical, approach to music and also to severely practical considerations. In the mission field—and the early days of European Christianity were essentially days of missionary effort—it was as well to

[33]

travel light. A priest intending to convert the heathen could hardly take with him a trained choir, even if one were available.

There was one basic problem that took a long time to solve. Since hymns and psalms and the music that had grown up with the words were regarded as sacred, it was essential that they should be formalized and that they should be performed in a uniform manner. To achieve such consistency schools of singing were established.

For practical purposes, we look back to the Benedictine monks of Monte Cassino, in Italy, who, after the destruction of their monastery by the Lombards, took refuge in Rome towards the end of the sixth century. Expert in singing, they attracted the attention of the the reforming Pope, Gregory "the Great", who was inspired by their example to set up schools of singing within the religious houses of Rome. These were houses which prepared students for the priesthood. Those who were gifted in singing were given an opportunity to develop their gifts, and soon there was a body not only of expert singers—who sang before the Pope on the great festivals—but also of teachers. In the seventh and eighth centuries singing teachers were sent from Rome to England, France, Germany, and Switzerland to improve the standard of church music in those countries, and also to supervise the establishment of more schools of singing.

Schools of singing were set up under the control of the church, and attached to monasteries and large churches. Since the church controlled all education and since it was of first importance to prepare boys from an early age for offices in the church, it was inevitable that the schools also cared for the musical education of the young. In the beginning, the development of music was hindered by the fact that teaching was necessarily by rote. All the songs and hymns had to be learned by ear, and memorized. Until there was some form of musical notation, music of a ritual nature was kept within fairly narrow limits. Until there was a proper system of notation any kind of complicated part singing was impracticable.

Music that is official—in this instance music of the church—is one side of music. The other is represented by "popular" music. In the Middle Ages this was folk music. Although the more strict among the church authorities looked on secular music with disapproval there were many in the church who were more tolerant. Consequently the gap between "sacred" and "secular" music was not as great as it was sometimes supposed to have been. Part singing was practised in folk music from very early times, and by the tenth century a similar kind of part music to that practised in folk music had begun to take its place in church music.

* The basis of part singing is the difference, already explained, of vocal registers. The simplest form of part singing, therefore, is that in which the same tune is sung by a number of people but with the pitch adjusted to suit particular registers. In this case, the tune will be in parallel lines—one line from one voice (or group of voices), one from another. This kind of singing tends to happen spontaneously, even now. We are all accustomed to the singer who cannot reach the high notes and sensibly avoids them, probably choosing notes an octave lower. In or about the tenth century, this natural, and sensible, practice was systematized. The kind of part singing then practised in the church belonged to male voices, and since, as we have seen, the tenor range is about five notes higher than the bass, the melody ran along parallel lines at this distance. This kind of singing—also familiar all over the world in the performance of folk music—was termed *organum*.

So far so good; but singers were not content to be restricted by the limitations of strict *organum*. They experimented, varying the pattern by extemporizing melodies that did not always go in the same direction as the main tune. At first there was one note in one part against a note of corresponding duration in the other part (or parts). But the time came when the rhythmic

[35]

structure was varied—with several notes in one part against one, longer, note in another part. Experiment of this and every other kind was rarely welcomed by the authorities of the church; but progress in the long run could not be halted. By the twelfth century choral music of a more or less complex character had firmly established itself in the liturgy of Western Europe. At the same time, there was also a strong and independent tradition of church music—based on the chants of the early Byzantine Church—in the Russian Orthodox church.

As the practical side of music developed so too did its scientific study. In the Middle Ages, a great deal was written on its theoretical and philosophic aspects. Regarding the latter, the only tenable proposition was that musical compositions were worthy when they were designed for, and performed in a manner acceptable to, God. So far as theory was concerned, this derived from the same principle. Thus the tonal system of the modes used for plainchant was made secure and composers worked within its limits. Differences between concord and discord were carefully defined and harmonic principles emerged. To some extent these principles were established by the laws of acoustics, which showed how from one sound others—known as harmonics—could be generated. In the simplest form this means that pieces began and ended with concords, and on the final note of whatever scale (in fact, then called "mode") was being used, or on the group of notes (or chord) naturally associated with that note. This sense of direction, implicit in any single line of melody, was essential to those who were singing in parts.

The more complex the texture of music became, the more it became necessary to regularize its rhythmic aspect. A singer likes to feel that he has a firm outline of rhythm on which he may depend, and this is afforded by metrical patterns. In plainsong the rhythm is supposed to be that of the words. In part singing—especially where there is a variety of note-lengths—word rhythms are not sufficiently precise. It was, then, a matter of common sense to institute a system in which the lengths of notes could be exactly related to one another. When such a system became established it was called the "mensural" system.

All these problems could only be solved by means of an acceptable form of musical notation. For many hundreds of years men had tried to discover methods by which sounds could be set down in such a way that they could be recognizable to the eye, and, therefore, interpreted into performance. In pre-Christian times, Egyptians, Greeks and Chinese had attempted to find symbols to represent sounds. In the Middle Ages, more or less independent efforts were made in various parts of Europe, but also in Persia, in Russia and even by the Buddhists of Tibet.

Notation grew from the fact of the rise and fall of melody. In the first place signs—or *neumes*—simply gave a general idea of rise and fall. The illustration below shows a page of a twelfth-century book of liturgical music used in the famous

Swiss school of singing at St. Gallen. It will be seen that the neumes above the Latin words look like so many accents—which serve a similar purpose to neumes. It was soon found more practicable to arrange symbols within a framework of lines and spaces, by which melodic intervals could be more easily calculated. In order to be easily recognizable, such symbols needed codification in regard to their actual relationship in sound. In short, sounds needed labels. There were two kinds of labels, both of which are still used. On the one hand, letters of the alphabet; on the other, names like those of sol-fa which could be memorized. The alphabetical method had long been applied to the writing down of symbols for sounds.

The sol-fa process was the brainwave of an Italian singing teacher of the twelfth century. By taking the syllables attached to the opening notes of successive phrases in a plainsong hymn, which conveniently made a rising scale, and by using these syllables as an aid to teaching his choristers the rudiments of musical theory, Guido d'Arezzo brought about a revolution in choir training. Thereafter, singers (who did enough practice), were enabled to know what they should be doing.

By the fourteenth century a form of notation in which signs showing relative pitch, the exact size of melodic intervals and the precise duration of sounds, was in general use throughout Europe. What had been achieved was described by various writers, among whom one of the most important was a French priest, Philippe de Vitry (1291–1361).

The four treatises by which de Vitry is remembered are known by the title of the first—*Ars Nova* (*The New Art*). From this we learn that many important developments had taken place by the middle of the fourteenth century.

Change in social and artistic affairs takes place gradually, but there are certain milestones in the process which are at least convenient for reference. At the time when *organum* was the regular method of singing in parts, the churches in which it was heard were built in the Romanesque style of architecture.

When Philippe de Vitry wrote his *Ars Nova* Romanesque architecture had everywhere been replaced by the more free and flowing style of Gothic. The age which saw the culmination of Gothic was also the age of such great poets as Dante, Petrarch, and Chaucer; of Boccaccio, one of the most famous of story tellers; of Giotto, the painter. All these great men brought into human affairs a new spirit of feeling for their fellowmen, of imaginative adventure and of artistic spontaneity. The same atmosphere pervaded the world of music. This was inevitable, because neither music nor any other art is an enclosure from which other aspects of life are excluded.

If you had gone into a monastery, a cathedral, or even a large town church, in almost any part of Europe in the mid-fourteenth century, you would have heard the ancient hymns and chants—sung in unison, and sometimes accompanied by organ and perhaps a variety of other instruments as well, or instead. You would have heard motets and masses in two, three and four parts, in all of which a foundation plainchant theme would be apparent. At Christmas you would have been able to see Nativity plays, with songs (or carols) for one or more parts as an integral part of the performance. At Easter and Whitsuntide, outside the church buildings, you would have seen Mystery and Miracle plays, which also contained a great deal of music—much of it of a more or less descriptive, or even dramatic, character. All these occurrences and occasions were linked together by song.

This is not all. Had you enjoyed the opportunity of visiting a palace—or possibly, the Abbot's Lodging in a religious house—you would have heard solo songs, in which the spirit of the love songs of the troubadours lived on, and folk songs and other songs of a popular character arranged so that they could be sung in parts. These part songs were also accompanied by instruments—especially by viols, recorders and lutes.

There is one famous and familiar piece of music for voices which not only survives from the thirteenth or fourteenth century but enjoys more popularity now than it ever did in the days in which it was composed. This is *Sumer is i-cumen in*, which belonged to the library of the monks at Reading, England. Monks? But this has nothing to do with church music, or so it seems. The words, lyrical and pastoral, are thoroughly secular. So is the infectious beat of the rhythm. But the manner in which the four upper voices follow each other with the same tune, above a repeated figure for two lower voices, is that in which music for church use was composed. The upper voices are in the form of a canon. The two lower voices are in the form known as *rondellus*. The only men with the scientific skill in composition required for such a work were those who had learned their technique in a church school of music. Fortunately, many of these men were far from stuffy. When they could, they entertained themselves with what were then described by the more austere as "worldly pleasures". In the fourteenth century the music of the world and the music of the cloister came together at several points.

The focal point of music is the performer. The fact that music widened its scope during the Middle Ages is due to the skills of those who were engaged in its practice just as much as to the intensive studies of the theorists. Those who were principally concerned with performance were the singers employed by the great churches—boys and men. The boys were generally restricted to the plainsong melodies, to singing in unison. Part singing was an occupation for men. For this there were two very good reasons. First of all, choristers were of necessity obliged to learn much of their music by rote—because there was as yet no printed music. The manuscripts, often very beautifully written and decorated, were few and precious. Secondly, part singing was at a formative stage, and the element of improvisation was, for a long time, an important factor. In all ways, then, it was not feasible to practise singing in parts unless only a few singers were involved.

Until well into the fifteenth century the more complex works for church use were sung by solo voices—one to a part. And the custom of having a few good singers rather than a larger group of less good ones was maintained in many famous institutions for a long time to come. The way in which choral bodies were composed, however, gave opportunity for varieties of texture and of tone colour. In the first place the unison singing (of boys, or of boys and men) could be contrasted with two- and three-part singing. That this was done in the fourteenth century is shown by the indications written into certain Italian manuscripts. In other Italian manuscripts of the early fifteenth century the instructions show that some sections of works were given to soloists, but others to the main body of singers which by now was singing in parts. The same kind of contrast occurs in English carols of the same date.

The first movement which may be considered fully choral— for more than a single singer to a part—is in a manuscript in Modena, Italy, which gives part of a setting of the story of the Passion of Christ. This part of the Christian record is the most dramatic, and since it was dramatized from an early point in the history of the medieval church, it became one of the starting points for secular drama. What is important is that it united the tradition of church music with a more popular tradition. The characters in the drama were not painted figures, but represented by living people. The Passion story demands the presence of a crowd, and the crowd adds its own comments. When these are set to music then it must be music for many singers. So it was in the manuscript at Modena. From that time until well on in the eighteenth century, "crowd music" was an important feature of musical settings of the Passion.

In addition to Nativity and Passion plays, there were liturgical dramas for Easter, for Whitsuntide, and occasionally for the Feast Days of particular saints. In Germany St. Gregory's Day (March 5) was marked by the performance of plays (not always of a strictly religious character) and, during the fourteenth and fifteenth centuries, music was provided not only by church

[41]

singers, but also those who belonged to brotherhoods or guilds, as well as by schoolboys. There was, therefore, a good deal of overlapping of sacred and secular.

So far as the development of techniques of choral music was concerned, however, this depended on the opportunities given to musicians employed by the church, or at the Court of a secular ruler. It should be pointed out that from the twelfth century kings (as well as dukes) increasingly maintained their own chapels, with a complete staff of clerics and musicians, as in a cathedral. The royal chapels also undertook the education of singing boys. At a secular court, the musicians were not as limited as in a cathedral or monastery. They were required not only to sing praises to God but also to the ruler, or simply to sing for the pleasure of the ruler and his guests.

Between the thirteenth and fifteenth centuries, great advances were made in the craft of musical composition as the result of the fruitful union of scientific and imaginative ideas within the art. The science of music concerns its acoustical nature and the principles arising from practices which may at any time be conveniently codified for the benefit of creative musicians in general. The principles of harmonic combination of sounds, for instance, arose from the phenomenon of harmonics or overtones generated by any single sound. The sounds we recognize as the common major chord are, in fact, the three most prominent harmonics. This is why the major common chord was accepted as a norm, and why its effectiveness was increasingly emphasized by the contrast either of the minor common chord or by more dissonant combinations.

In the song *Sumer is i-cumen in* the basic form of the composition is imitative. When one voice follows another with the same tune the result as has been seen, is a *canon*, or at least canonic. In a quodlibet of a rough-and-ready kind it doesn't much matter whether discord and concord are placed schematically. In a musical work designed to take its place among other works of art it does matter. The higher forms of art are marked

[42]

by a sense of order. Throughout the period under consideration the search for order went on, and was in large measure based on the placing of discord in relation to concord. This is where the imaginative process comes in to help the creative artist to make the best possible use of the scientific principles so far accepted.

It would, however, be wrong to see the "scientist" on one side, and the "artist" on the other. It so happens that an early and influential figure in the history of choral music was, literally, both scientist and artist. This was the Englishman, John Dunstable (d. 1435), astronomer, mathematician, and musician. Very little is known about Dunstable's life, except that at some time he was in the service of the Duke of Bedford, who was Regent in France from 1422–35.

In those days, as during the preceding century, there were close, not always friendly, connections between England and France. From the point of view of music, however, the connection produced admirable results in a pooling of resources. French musicians learned from English musicians, and vice versa. This was particularly the case in respect of the two Chapels Royal, the members of which were often on speaking terms when their masters were not. In those days, because of the conformity imposed by a common church and the universal use of Latin in the liturgy, music was more international than in any subsequent period. Where a musician came from did not matter; what kind of a musician he was did matter.

So far as is known Dunstable, as well as a number of his English contemporaries, spent the greater part of his working life in Europe, and all his existing works are only to be found in continental libraries. Apart from two or three secular songs, they are all liturgical; sections of the Mass and motets. In these, the basis is invariably a plainsong theme, but often treated with a considerable freedom. The manner in which fragments of traditional themes were varied reminds us of the later and familiar pattern of "air and variations". The voice,

[43]

not the highest voice, to which the motivating theme was given was called the *tenor*, for the simple reason that this was the "holding" part. During the fourteenth century, particularly in France, the tenor theme was divided up into matching rhythmic sections, around which the other parts were constructed. The basis of such a structure was rhythmic rather than melodic, and attitudes to musical composition were strongly mathematical.

John Dunstable studied the strict and mathematical methods of the French composers Philippe de Vitry and Guillaume Machaut (d. 1377), but he was more inventive and more flexible. In England there was a long and well-known tradition of concordant singing and Dunstable brought together the kind of harmonies peculiar to England, and the kind of rhythms that dominated the French style. Moreover he began to envisage works of larger proportions, consisting of separate movements bound together by common musical themes.

The Service of the Mass was and is the centre of Catholic worship. It was customary to set to music five sections of the Mass: the Kyrie eleison, the Gloria, the Credo, the Sanctus, and the Agnus Dei. Although these were performed at particular points during the service, and were separated from one another, there was a tendency for musicians to think of the five sections as a unified whole. This was emphasized by the growing use of a common plainsong theme. The example shown on the following page, from one of Dunstable's Masses, gives the beginning of the plainsong in the lowest part (Ex. 5).

There are now no more than about sixty pieces by Dunstable in existence. His reputation, however, was kept alive by the praise bestowed on him by those who followed and admired his music.

French, Flemish and Spanish musicians and writers paid tribute to Dunstable. One of them, the Fleming Joannes de Tinctoris, (about 1446 to about 1511), tells us a little about contrasting styles of singing. English singing of that period, he

beginning of plainsong theme, carried on in lower part.

EX. 5

said, was rough in comparison with French singing, which was characterized by neatness and precision. But the English singing was more free. (It is not quite clear of what this freedom consisted. But one may suppose that the English were more inclined to add extempore ornamentation whenever possible.)

During the greater part of the fourteenth century the Pope's headquarters were not in Rome, but in the Provençal city of Avignon. Towards the end of the century, the Pope moved back to Rome, but for some time rival Popes resided in Avignon. The last of them was removed in 1408. After this situation had been cleared up, it was important to re-establish the authority of the Papacy in every way. There was, therefore, a re-invigoration of music at St. Peter's Basilica. It depended more on non-Italian than on Italian musicians.

In France and Flanders, much money had been invested in the musical establishments of court and church, and the singers and composers of those countries were renowned throughout Europe. A succession of Popes enticed some of the best musicians to Rome, with the result that by the end of the fifteenth century some of the best singing was to be heard there. Tinctoris, named above, was a Papal singer for some time; so also was Guillaume Dufay (d. 1474).

Born in Flanders about the beginning of the fifteenth century, Dufay became a choirboy in the cathedral in Cambrai. In those days the occupation of choirboy was much sought after by

[45]

ambitious parents on behalf of their sons. For those who were not wealthy, it afforded almost the only opportunity for a proper education. Boys in the choir schools were instructed in the ordinary curriculum which could qualify them in due course to become priests or officials (the two callings were often the same). But they were also given an all-round musical training. In an important cathedral there was also an opportunity of attracting the interest and patronage of the influential. Dufay was successful on all fronts.

As a young man, he was enabled to go to Italy (where he wrote some secular songs for a family by whom he may have been employed). He studied, it is thought, at the University of Bologna, and in 1428 became a member of the Papal Choir. He held this post for ten years, during which he established not only his own reputation as a musician but also that of his countrymen.

Because we are not able to know exactly what any piece of music sounded like at this period, we have to take it on trust that it moved people just as much as any music of more recent times. We cannot appreciate from a painting the actual sound of music; but we can appreciate what the painter thought about it. Simon Marmion (d. 1489) was a Franco-Flemish painter contemporary with Dufay. In his beautiful painting, *Choir of Angels* (part of a panel), he shows singers and trumpeters performing together (see also the instrumentalists and singers on the picture opposite). This conveys at least a feeling. And the singers were practical people who preferred to get the notes right by reading from the music. No doubt where they were they *had* to get the notes right!

3

The Splendours of Rome

WHEN Guillaume Dufay joined the Papal choir, called the Sistine Choir after the name of the Sistine Chapel in which it usually performed, there were twenty-four members. It had lately been increased from the previous number of twelve singers—about the average for any moderately-sized cathedral or abbey throughout Europe. The treble (soprano) and, perhaps, the alto parts were supplied by boys' voices. By now, copies of the music to be sung being more readily available than formerly and details of notation having been standardized, boys could take a full part in the performance of polyphonic music.

It was the custom for the adult members of the Sistine Choir —each a composer as well as a singer—to provide practically all the music that was required for the normal services and also for many extra ceremonial occasions. The choir worked on a kind of democratic principle. When a motet or Mass had been composed, the composer would produce a rough copy so that his colleagues could sing it through. If there was general agreement that the new music was worthy of inclusion in the repertoire, a fair copy was made. Four full-time copyists were employed, and they were kept permanently busy.

The Flemish painter, Marten de Vos (1532–1603) of Antwerp, and the engraver Johann Sadeler (who worked in Brussels, 1550, and in Venice, 1600) were well-placed to become acquainted with the great Italo-Flemish choral tradition. They

recorded it in considerable detail—within a heightened baroque idiom—in paintings and engravings. In the illustration shown above a customary choir of angels is shown performing a Nativity hymn (in nine parts, with one singer to a part). It would appear, however, that not all the choristers were concentrating on their music. In the next illustration a group of Chapel Royal singers (at the Court of King Solomon supposedly) are singing a motet by the Flemish composer Andreas Pevernage (1543–91) of which the words are taken from the *Song of Solomon*. It may be thought that these words are not

very suitable for church use. They were, none the less, set by many composers, including Palestrina. The four parts lie before the singers in one huge part-book. Such a book is typical of the period, and it can be seen that the copyist made a good job of this piece. Many such books were compiled all over

EX. 6

Europe and often they were beautifully decorated. The opening of this particular motet is given in the example above, where the original clefs are shown as well as their modern counterparts (Ex. 6).

Between 1471 and 1484, during the reign of Pope Sixtus IV, the Sistine Choir was again enlarged; this time to thirty-two singers. A keen music lover himself, the Pope gave the choir every opportunity to appear in public. It should be remembered that the Popes of the sixteenth and seventeenth centuries were not very different from secular rulers and that their tastes and recreations were by no means limited by their sacred calling. They chased culture (and pleasure) as avidly as the next man, and rarely showed any inclination to appear backward in respect to the artistic aims of the period. Ceremonies, therefore, were splendidly organized, and much enhanced by fine music. Sometimes the music was rearranged for instruments so that it could be enjoyed away from the ceremonies themselves.

Another great Flemish musician of the fifteenth century was Jean de Okeghem (his name is spelled in many different ways!). Okeghem (about 1420 to about 1495) was a chorister at Antwerp. He spent most of his career in France, where he became director of the music of the Royal Chapel. One of his pupils was Josquin des Prés (about 1445–1521), who was employed at various Italian courts before becoming a member of the Papal Choir in 1486. After a period of activity in Rome he returned north, working in France, the Netherlands, and Vienna, depending on who was prepared to offer him the best contracts. Josquin, whose reputation was higher than that of any other musician of his time, composed Masses on the one hand, and "chansons" (part songs) on the other. He also acted as a talent scout, and the Duke of Ferrara met him in 1501 in Flanders signing on singers for employment in Italy.

Jacob Obrecht (about 1450–1505) was a dominant figure in the musical life of Flanders, being at various times director of music at Cambrai, Bruges and Antwerp, before succumbing to the temptation of the warmer climate and better rewards of Italy. Towards the end of his life he was appointed musician to the Medici family at Ferrara. At an earlier stage of his career

[51]

he had been given six months' leave of absence by his Flemish employers to assist in the musical affairs of the Medicis.

Obrecht was a composer whose influence was widespread. A setting of the Passion, ascribed to him, achieved considerable popularity. Composed in the style of a motet, for four voices, it was especially welcome in Germany, where the Passion was enacted and sung in many towns and villages. There is a copy of Obrecht's *Passion* in existence, in which a musician at the Court of Meiningen, has written a German translation over the Latin text. Many German composers took Obrecht's work as an example when writing Passion settings. He was also among the first composers whose works were published.

The earliest printed music dates from 1473, when a book of plainsong was issued in Southern Germany. In the next twenty years great progress was made both by German and Italian printers. The most famous of the early printers was Ottaviano dei Petrucci (1466–1539), who was given a licence by the City of Venice to set up as a printer of music in 1501. Venice was a music-loving city, and the authorities were as quick to see the possibilities inherent in the publication of music, as was Petrucci. In all he issued sixty-one collections of music, both sacred and secular, which included representative works by the principal composers of the day. These included Obrecht, Josquin des Prés, Okeghem, Heinrich Isaac (about 1450–1517), Alexander Agricola (d. about 1506), Pierre de la Rue (d. 1518) and others. The effect of such publication was, of course, tremendous. Just as the printing of books led to a general awakening of interest in new ideas, so did the printing of music lead to a broad appreciation of new ideas in music. The full effect, however, as in the case of literature, was some way off.

It should be said that when music in parts was printed, the parts were shown separately, and not as nowadays in a score which gives one part above another so that all may be read simultaneously. The sixteenth-century singer followed his own part. One hopes that he listened to the rest. Despite the fact

[52]

that by now music was printed, there were several refinements to come. For, as yet, there were no bar lines to guide the eye, and there were no expression marks to help the manner of performance (see illustration on p. 71).

To sing music that has no bar lines requires a precise grasp of time values. Remembering that the music of the fifteenth century had a close connection with mathematics, especially in the universities, and that it was regarded as a branch of science (as science was then known), it must be accepted that exactness in interpreting the time factor had the highest priority. A strict interpretation goes against later ideas of expressiveness. In the period with which we are dealing, however, *our* idea of expression did not apply. This partly explains why marks of expression did not appear in the first printed books of music— nor for a long time to come.

The case, however, is not as simple as this. To think that music was once performed without variety of tone, without contrast between loud and soft, is nonsense. This we know since throughout the Middle Ages there were many references (mostly by eminent, but conservative, clergymen who did not like what they heard) to different styles of singing. In at least one very early manuscript there were indications to show which sections should be soft and which should be loud. But these were matters usually left to the discretion of the individual choirmaster. Tone and dynamic contrast are inherent in the art of singing. What is not, is the direct relationship later evolved between details of musical structure (the work of the individual composer) and details of verbal expression. It may seem obvious to us that a sombre mood is best conveyed in a minor tonality. It did not seem obvious to the fifteenth-century composer—for the simple reason that he did not know of minor and major tonalities. He was still using the system of modes or scales that had come down to him as part of the "package deal" that was Gregorian music.

But things were changing, and changing rapidly. Church music was essentially functional. It had its own place in liturgical

[53]

order apart from which it had no valid independent existence. In the fifteenth century, men did not go to St. Peter's, Rome, with the intention of hearing a new work by Guillaume Dufay, because they particularly wished to hear music by him. It is even doubtful if the great majority ever thought of asking who the composer of the day's Mass was. Music, like paintings, sculptures, stained-glass windows, the vestments of the priests, the altar-cloths and hangings of the church, was there and unquestioned.

Composers, however, formed a close corporation. They belonged to the learned class, and they took pride in their skills. Thus they employed their skills for their mutual satisfaction, developing the involved, intellectual style that characterized the Flemish school. The music of Dufay and Okeghem, for example, is full of contrapuntal ingenuity, in the interweaving of parts, in the use of imitation, and in the exploitation of the device of canon. To our ears this music may seem cold, because the chords lack the richness of later music, and because we have grown accustomed to harmonic conventions attained at a different time and in different circumstances. The same music may also seem somewhat lacking in meaning because the Latin words do not fit the musical notes as we would.expect.

But if we pass on to listen to the works of des Prés, even more to those of Obrecht, we will note that the rhythm is often simplified. We may well also feel that the harmony is richer because major and minor chords are accepted as normal. The music falls into clearer sections because of the emphasis placed on the final notes, or cadences. Finally there often seems more purpose in the music because it conveys the character of the words.

At the beginning of the Middle Ages a composer wrote very little secular music. At the end, he wrote a good deal. In the thirteenth and fourteenth centuries the two kinds of music, secular and sacred, had come together, in spite of the official disapproval of "worldly" music by the church. By the beginning of the sixteenth century—in spite of objections by the pious—there was, so far as style was concerned, hardly any difference between them. If there was, it lay in the fact that the "chansons", sometimes arrangements of folk songs, were less complicated in structure than the motets to which, in general, they corresponded. Rhythmically speaking they were more direct, more in line with dance.

At this point we find differences of function. Secular music, whether the "chanson", the madrigal which evolved from it, or the instrumental piece (an arrangement of vocal music, or of folk dance), was less directed at the highly-trained professional church, or court musician, than at the enthusiastic amateur. The latter at least could try out his talents—often expensively developed under a private tutor—in "chanson" or its allied forms, or in the dances for viols or wind instruments that were coming into fashion. Secular music was composed with one eye on the amateur. Church music was strictly for trained performers.

The amateurs of music in the Renaissance, however keen they were on music, were primarily interested in literature. The story of music from the middle fifteenth to the early seventeenth centuries is the record of a change of alliance. Music loosened its scientific connections somewhat and came into a more reciprocal arrangement with poetry and drama. During this time, the poet had something to say about the relationship between the two arts. Not unnaturally, he emphasized that *his* work was just as important as that of the composer, and that the latter should pay due regard to the fact. This, in brief, encouraged a new kind of musical expression; and, eventually, new kinds of music.

Meanwhile the Flemings maintained their dominant position in Europe. Of the composers named on p. 52 Pierre de la Rue was a pupil of Okeghem, as also was Alexander Agricola. Heinrich Isaac was either Flemish or German by birth, but a master of the styles developed by the Netherlanders. All three composers, however, were European, rather than national figures, at home in Italy, France, Spain, or almost any other part of the then Holy Roman Empire. The climax of the Flemish school was reached with Adrian Willaert (about 1480–1562) and Orlandus Lassus (1532–94).

Willaert held a number of appointments, of which the most important was that of director of music in St. Mark's Cathedral, Venice. Here he developed a song school which was to be one of the most influential in Italy, because the combination of instruments with voices was specially cultivated. Willaert, like all musicians of strong imagination, exploited the particular conditions of the building in which he worked. In St. Mark's Cathedral there were two choirs, and two organs. Willaert found it effective to use the two forces, both together and in contrast with one another. This led to the composition of music for double choir. He went even further and his contemporaries were entranced by a setting of the *Magnificat* for three choirs.

Although he spent a great deal of his time directing and composing church music, Willaert also wrote instrumental music and a large number of madrigals.

Orlandus Lassus is, beyond doubt, one of the world's greatest composers. Of those who lived in the sixteenth century he was the one who most seemed to anticipate the future of musical experience, because his works often appear to reflect shades of emotion. This is not altogether surprising since the capacity of music to depict the values inherent in words and the character of natural phenomena was becoming increasingly a matter for discussion at that time. There were many reasons for this. On the one hand, there were—especially in Italy—many societies, of which the members were a cultural minority of the aristocracy, devoted to the study of intellectual and artistic questions. On the other, the revolutionary forces that had convulsed Europe (as described in the next chapter) had greatly affected attitudes to music and the principles underlying its composition. Lassus was a great European figure. He worked in Italy, his most important post being that of choirmaster of the Church of St. John Lateran in Rome, where a school of music had been established in 1535. Lassus travelled a good deal. He appears to have been briefly in England in 1554, and his travels are reflected in his ability to use a number of languages. Some of his letters are still in existence—they are the first significant letters from a composer to have been preserved —and they were written sometimes in Latin, sometimes in French, sometimes in Italian, and sometimes in German.

The music of Lassus also reflects this kind of universality. He composed German, and French, part songs, many in four parts; settings of poems by Petrarch in the form of madrigals; motets, Masses, Passion settings, and other Catholic church music, as well as arrangements of Lutheran chorales (or hymns). This great range of music is characterized by a technique which was so diversified as to be able to indicate many aspects of human feeling. The popular songs of Lassus, especially those in the Italian villanella style, which was close to folk music, are distinguished by lightness and humour. Church music of a solemn nature is often marked by a sense of tragedy. In the latter case, Lassus expounded the melodic and harmonic quality of musical expression by making bold use of *chromatic* notes (notes which do not belong to the particular mode or scale being used, and requiring accidentals in the notation).

From 1557 until his death, Lassus lived in Munich, as director of music to the Duke of Bavaria. His works were published in many places, including Venice, Rome, Antwerp, Paris, Munich and Nürnberg. In 1588 two part songs by Lassus were printed in the famous English collection of madrigals, *Musica Transalpina* (see p. 88).

During the period in which Flemish composers' music enjoyed pre-eminence in Europe, choral music underwent many changes. These changes took place gradually, but works composed towards the end of the sixteenth century sound different from those composed at the beginning of the century. The later works are more varied in character; the plainsong melodies, although still frequently used as a basis for Mass and motet composition, are treated more flexibly. Contrapuntal movement, still the foundation of choral music, is less mathematical, and more exactly calculated to the progress of chordal patterns in a harmonic framework. The old modal system, now no longer so restricted, is beginning to change, so that music of the later sixteenth century appears to be within earshot of the tonal structure of classical times.

The remarkable achievements of the great Flemings should not be allowed to blot out the fact that choral music was strong in every European country, and each had its own composers. Not least of all was this the case in Italy. The emergence of a "school" of composers obviously depends on the individual talents of the members of that "school". But it also depends on opportunity.

Renaissance Italy was a land of opportunity. The fact that dukes and princes, each governing his own domain, were rich and strongly interested in the arts acted as a great stimulus to secular music-making. When poetry and music met together, the madrigal was born. The church in Italy was also affected by the general movement of Renaissance thought, with the result that church music was less confined by doctrinaire considerations than was formerly the case. Although it would not have been officially admitted, music in church became almost an end in itself. Certainly foreign visitors more and more went to St. Peter's in Rome, or St. Mark's in Venice, simply to hear, and to wonder at the music.

The tradition of giving the chief places in the field of church music to French and Fleming musicians declined in the sixteenth century when native Italian composers showed a disinclination to take second place. Two key figures in the changeover from Flemish to Italian domination in Catholic church music were Andrea Gabrieli (about 1510–86) and Giovanni Pierluigi da Palestrina (1525–95). The former, a pupil of Willaert, spent his life in the service of St. Mark's, Venice (as also did his famous nephew, Giovanni). The latter worked most of his life in Rome, where he became regarded as the supreme composer of the establishment. Gabrieli, influenced by the lively Venetian tradition, looked to the future; Palestrina summed up the great Medieval–Renaissance tradition of vocal music in parts. With justice, he is regarded as one of the greatest of all composers of church choral music.

Palestrina, who took the name of the Italian town where he was born, began as a choirboy. He had the good fortune to be able to continue his musical education in Rome at the Church of St. Maria Maggiore, where the Bishop of Palestrina had been appointed archpriest. This church was another of the Roman foundations in connection with which a song-school had been founded at the beginning of the sixteenth century. Palestrina spent some time as organist in his native town, before being appointed director of the Julian Choir. This was in 1550. Four years later he became a member of the Papal, the Sistine, Choir. For the rest of his life, Palestrina lived and worked in Rome, where he gradually acquired a position of great authority. He became director of music at St. John Lateran in 1555, in succession to Lassus, of St. Maria Maggiore in 1561, and of a new training school for priests, founded in 1565. In 1570 he once again took over the Julian Choir.

Biographies of great men are often distorted by writers whose love of romance is stronger than their concern for facts. Palestrina has always been a godsend to writers of this kind, as is shown by this account written into a collection of his music compiled in England in the mid-eighteenth century:

The following Anecdote was communicated to me by a Friend from Doctor Pepusch. He was first taken notice of by Rinaldo dell Mell [who was a pupil of Palestrina!], who walking in the streets of Rome, heard Palestina [written so], then a poor ragged Boy singing and begging his bread. Discovering something of a more than ordinary Genius in the

Boy, he took him home, cloath'd, educated and instructed him in his Profession, which was that of Music, in which he was of the first note. In this Palestrina made a remarkable Proficiency, very soon excelling his Master. A Monk, or Friar, being accquainted [written so] with his Merit, recommended him to the Pope's notice, who had for some time banished Music from his Chapell upon account of the levity usual in Composition. His Holiness gave him some Peices [written so] to set, which he did with such a religious solemnity, and in so masterly a manner, that he was pleased to appoint him Maestro di Capella. (Brit. Mus. Add. Ms 31398.)

Nevertheless the truth was that Palestrina became the most important musician in the church in Rome, and, therefore, the principal figure in the field of Catholic church music. Palestrina had the ear of the Pope and he was highly regarded by successive holders of that office. Among these were Julius III, to whom Palestrina dedicated his first volume of Masses in 1554; Marcellus II, whose name stands in the title of a famous Mass by Palestrina; Gregory XIII, who asked the composer to revise the music of the Roman liturgy; and Sixtus V, by whom Palestrina was acknowledged to be the chief of the Papal singers. Palestrina also dedicated a volume of Masses to Philip II, of Spain.

During this period, the whole position of the church in the (then) modern world was under serious consideration. It was the age of the Reformation. To recover from the shock that this had caused at the hitherto unquestioned capital of Western Christendom, the Roman church authorities needed to try to put their own house in order. The measures taken—largely as a result of the Council of Trent—included some revision of attitudes to the subject of music in worship. Reform in this particular meant on the one hand a stricter regard for the traditional, plainsong, music of the liturgy, and on the other a demand for a simpler kind of choral music.

As it happened, Palestrina himself had evolved a style that was less needlessly complicated than that of some of the earlier Flemish composers. While no less a master of counterpoint than his predecessors, Palestrina avoided any form of intellectual exhibitionism and evolved a style that was, and remains, a model of clarity and proportion. Palestrina's surviving works number nearly 1,000, among which are ninety-three Masses, some 600 motets or compositions in motet style, and 200 madrigals. Of the latter, four were published in England in *Musica Transalpina* in 1588.

Palestrina composed music for groups of anything from four to twelve separate parts, and it is marked by its pure, vocal quality. There is, perhaps, no single work by this remarkable composer in which any part is not immediately singable. Three centuries after it had been written Claude Debussy (1862–1918) heard a Mass by Palestrina in a small church in Rome, where he was a student at the time. He also heard a Mass by Lassus. He described both composers as "masters", and wrote in a letter to a friend: "You perhaps don't know that counterpoint can be the nastiest thing in music, but in their work it is beautiful."

In the Sistine Chapel the tradition was, and is, of unaccompanied singing—*a cappella* singing, that is. The idea that all polyphonic music of the sixteenth and seventeenth centuries was sung in this way is false. More often than not voices were supported by instruments—by organ, or by strings with or without wind instruments. The ideal of Catholic church music, however, was music for the human voice alone.

Palestrina's career came at the end of the long period of exclusive Roman supremacy, and that he was the composer who most of all summarized the character of polyphonic music as it had developed over many centuries, and that he was acknowledged as a very great composer, put him in a unique historical position. He became the great exponent of the tradition of classical church music to later generations, and, within the

Catholic church, the defender of the musical faith. No musical historian since the sixteenth century has dared to omit to praise Palestrina as a musician; and no Pope, or other dignitary of the Roman Catholic church, has failed to pay tribute to his music.

Many composers adopted the Palestrina style, and among those who exported it was Giovanni Francesco Anerio (about 1567–1621) who was for a time musician to King Sigismund III in Poland. Later he returned to Rome. Anerio left a fine setting of the special Mass for the Dead (*Requiem Mass*). The way in which this work grows from a plainsong theme is shown in the following example. It will also be seen how the voices enter one after the other, in imitation—the most characteristic feature of the style of the period (Ex. 7.)

4

Martin Luther and Music

ALTHOUGH this is a book about choral music there has as yet been no kind of group of singers resembling what we would now recognize as a "choral society". Until the sixteenth century the practice of singing the finest examples of music for voices had been reserved for the professionals of the best church choirs, for aristocratic amateurs or for those who were engaged by the aristocrats to entertain them. During the sixteenth century, Europe was convulsed by a sequence of events which combined to break into many kinds of privilege. The Reformation has already been mentioned in passing, but in many lands the religious upheaval of the time was also accompanied by civil disturbances, as underprivileged people tried to assert their rights. Few men of that age were more important than the great German reformer, Martin Luther (1483–1546), who may justly be regarded as the founder of the modern choral society.

Luther destroyed the Pope's claim to have the right to control the spiritual beliefs and practices of the whole of Europe. He also destroyed much of the authority of the Holy Roman Emperor. Luther insisted on the importance of the Bible being in the language of the people and not in Latin. By translating it into German, he emphasized the dignity of the speech used by ordinary people in everyday affairs. Luther made the German language a literary medium, and in so doing, helped to quicken a sense of national pride among those (living in various states) for whom German was their mother tongue.

The two institutions that were most radically changed, as a result of Luther's Reformation, were the church and the school. In the church, the minister became less important than the individual member of the congregation. In the school, the teacher was face-to-face with a new challenge—to make his pupils learn to master their own language and to give them a new sense of idealism. In all of this, music had an important function.

Luther not only loved music, he was a capable, practical, musician. He played the lute and, as a student in the University of Erfurt, had the reputation of being a good singer. He had once been a choirboy and had learned to take his part in the performance of the motets and Masses of Josquin des Prés, Orlandus Lassus, and other famous masters. This music meant a great deal to him, and he was averse to its passing out of use. In the pre-Reformation church there was, he said, much music that was good, and what was good should be retained.

On the other hand, there was the music of the common people. Luther knew and loved the folk songs and other popular songs of Germany, which he also considered to be of great value. Within the Lutheran Church, then, he aimed to bring together the best of the two traditions. He was a poet, and composed poems for hymns which were to be the rallying point of his church. Sometimes he wrote words to fit an existing folk song; sometimes he composed original tunes for his hymns; sometimes he invited other musicians to provide the music. In this way he established the type of popular hymn known as the *chorale*. Of all Lutheran chorales the most famous is *Ein feste Burg (A sure stronghold)*.

The chorale was Luther's great contribution to German music. Intended for the masses, it was a means of conveying religious principles. But, by making use of the inborn love of music and by demanding the exercise of skill, it encouraged a belief in individual talent. Luther wanted chorales to be sung, and to be sung well. And he insisted that they should be set and sung in parts.

It is fortunate that Luther was a close friend of many excellent musicians, who shared his ideals. Among them the most important were Johan Walther (1496–1570) and Georg Rhau (about 1488–1548). Walther, a singer in the choir of the Elector of Saxony, helped Luther to organize the music for the Lutheran Liturgy in 1524, and he spent the rest of his life in working towards the realization of Luther's ideals. He composed and arranged chorales; he re-established the Elector's choir; he taught music in the school at Torgau, where Luther's son was a pupil. Georg Rhau was the Cantor of St. Thomas's School in Leipzig (the office later held by J. S. Bach) before he came to Wittenberg to help Luther. He was not only a practising musician but also a publisher, and from Wittenberg he issued many collections of chorales, as well as other music, and books about music.

Rhau supplied a steady demand for music for singing, which came from the schools. He emphasized constantly that his publications were particularly designed for use in schools. This, perhaps, was the reason why the chorale asserted itself so triumphantly. It was also a chief factor in making the musical tradition of Germany, in later times, the envy of the rest of the world.

In no other educational system was music taken so seriously, or given so much importance, as in that which developed from Luther's ideas. Philip Melanchthon (1497–1560)—a fine scholar who also worked with Luther, and with the musicians at Wittenberg—drew up a scheme which was adopted in those states where the ruler was a Lutheran. Music in the German schools had to be in the hands of a trained musician—who was also expected to be able to teach other subjects (Latin, or religious instruction). If, as in a small village, there was only one teacher, he was expected to be competent to take charge

[65]

of the music. There was music in the timetable for each day, but there was also a great deal of music outside school hours.

Music lessons were generally given in German schools during the hour following the midday break on at least four days in the week. Boys learned the traditional plainsong melodies that were taken over from the old Catholic liturgy into the Lutheran service, and the chorales. They were sometimes taught by rote, but also frequently by means of the sol-fa system, as it was then understood. They learned to read at sight as soon as possible. In schools where the musical life was enriched by close association with a church in which the music was of a high standard boys learned to sing in the polyphonic music of the older masters described in the previous chapter. This was the case not only in important towns but even in small villages. Such works were kept in precious volumes that had been carefully copied by industrious cantors. A book of this kind, from which Martin Luther and Johann Sebastian Bach had sung during their school days, is still preserved in the archives of the town of Eisenach, where Bach was born and where Luther had been a schoolboy.

Boys who were trained to sing such music were required to practise after school hours. They provided, in fact, the treble and alto parts in the church choirs of the period. Those whose voices had "broken"—if they retained serviceable voices—were promoted to the tenor and bass sections, where they joined masters and other male adult members of the community.

The boys who belonged to the church choirs of post-Reformation Germany had to work hard, in accordance with the ancient practice that prevailed in the pre-Reformation church, and which had not been disturbed by the reformers. Their mistakes were corrected by corporal punishment. But they also had privileges. First, they were paid for their work. Then, at Christmas and New Year they were allowed to sing for money in the streets, in front of the houses of the wealthier citizens. They were engaged to sing at weddings, funerals, and civic functions. School drama flourished and choral items were invariably introduced into plays. While in some towns the old Mystery Plays—that had been such a feature of medieval town life—continued into the late sixteenth century. In Freiberg, in Saxony, where the plays were very famous, such performances took place outside the "Golden Porch" of the Cathedral. The choirboys of the Grammar School sang motets and chorales regularly. The audience joined in the singing of the chorales. A charming part song in cradle-song idiom of the sixteenth century, for three voices, by an unknown Thuringian composer, has all the atmosphere of the Nativity plays that were once so popular (Ex. 8).

EX. 8

The two most famous choirs in Germany at that time were in Leipzig and Dresden. The Leipzig choir belonged to the Church of St. Thomas, where a choral foundation was first established in the year 1213. The Dresden choir, founded at about the same time, was attached to the Church of the Holy Cross, and was, therefore, known as the *Kreuzchor* ("Choir of the Cross"). In the course of time, the institutions in which these boys were educated became boarding schools and, after the Reformation, boys were drawn from far and wide. These two choirs, which are still active, became the centres of some of the most important developments in German choral music. In the sixteenth and seventeenth centuries, there were other boarding schools from which choristers were drawn, especially in northern Germany, in Lüneburg and Hamburg.

The important place occupied by music in the educational

system led to the publication of text-books useful to teachers. Those that were issued—especially *Rudiments of Music* (1539), by Martin Agricola, and *Introduction to Music* (1550), Heinrich Faber—in the first half of the sixteenth century were written in Latin. A little later such books, of which there was a regular flood, were more helpfully written in German.

Singing in parts was considered to be the aim which every singer should set for himself. Martin Luther advised that it should be encouraged in schools. At the back of his mind was the old idea that part singing was the most perfect form of music with which to praise God. But he and his advisers also believed that such exercise was a fine discipline which influenced every other branch of learning. Part singing taught precision and independence, helped an appreciation of language, and encouraged co-operation and social well-being.

Behind this, however, lay another factor. Martin Luther brought the German language to maturity, and the chorales composed in the sixteenth century were symbols of this maturity. By singing them regularly, boys (and adults) unconsciously developed a sense of pride in their language and in their country. It is wrong to speak of nationalism in any modern sense in this connection, but the singing lessons of the sixteenth and seventeenth centuries did help to promote ideas in the community that were later to be recognized as nationalistic.

The development of this type of musical education was not altogether new, but the continuation of a tradition that had—as in the cases of the Leipzig and Dresden choirs—been there for a long time. As a result of Lutheran reform and extension of existing practices, the song school (part of the grammar school, and usually controlled by the town council) was brought into close touch with popular music. The love of the German-speaking people for music was very deep-seated, and secular music societies had been in existence since the fifteenth century. These were organized by the Trade Guilds and were described as societies of "Mastersingers". The Mastersingers of Nürnberg was the most famous of such societies and formed the theme for the most lively and entertaining of Richard Wagner's operas. Similar societies were formed in a number of towns. The silver miners of Freiberg, for example, had their own guild of Mastersingers. But they were not as competition-minded as the Mastersingers of Nürnberg and were content to function rather more as a choral society, which continued to exist right down to the late nineteenth century.

In 1526, Luther's friend Johann Walther, was director of music in Torgau, where the Elector of Saxony had a palace. As musical adviser to Luther and the music-loving Elector, as well as Cantor in the school, Walther had a position of some authority. When he suggested the formation of a town choral society in Torgau he did not have much trouble in finding recruits. A choral society was formed and was called a "Kantorei". Supported partly by the town council and partly by the Elector (both of whom had representatives on its governing committee), the "Kantorei" got off to a good start. Within a short time there were hundreds of such groups all over Germany. As modern choral societies do, they sang both secular and sacred music; and they devoted a good deal of attention to the social side. Particular members of the committee, for instance, looked after the food and drink that were consumed at meetings of the members.

In the German towns there were groups of woodwind and string musicians available. They were appointed by the town council, or by the local duke or count. Sometimes they were engaged by the town and the local ruler. From early times these musicians had played from the towers of churches, the balconies of town halls, and in the precincts of the castles, as and when required. In the sixteenth century—and even more in the seventeenth century—these instrumentalists were, from time to time, engaged to collaborate both with the church choirs and the choral societies. This was to have important results.

[69]

The kind of music that is created in any community at any time is determined not only by the condition of musical knowledge, but by the way in which people live and think. Martin Luther gave a particular pattern to German music, but that this pattern was effectively maintained for a matter of 200 years was due to the way in which the German States were governed. At the head of each one was an Elector, a Duke, or a Count—whose word was law. Without exception, these heads of state were prepared to support "culture", because of the effect such support had on their own reputations. This, of course, was true in many other parts of Europe. But the Protestant German rulers had a greater control over church affairs, so that sacred choral music was very much a matter of concern to the ruler. For the musician, what was important was that funds were generally forthcoming to subsidize his activities.

The situation was a curious and an involved one. Most German towns had one or more town choirs, and also a group of instrumental musicians. But within the palace of the local ruler, there was another body of musicians, appointed to sing and to play in the Court Chapel and also in the reception-rooms of the ruler, whenever he wished to entertain guests. In general, however, duties overlapped, so that the best of the town musicians often performed at the Court, and vice versa. So it was that there was as much music as anyone could have wished for.

The demand for new music, therefore, was very great. Since every properly-trained cantor, or organist, or "Kapellmeister" (leader of a musical establishment, known as a "Kapelle"), was a composer there was a great flood of new music after the Lutheran Reformation. The Germans played a large part in the invention of printing, and were also pioneers in the engraving of music. Throughout the sixteenth century, and afterwards, music books for singers came off the presses in profusion. The title page of the tenor part of a collection of part songs published in Nürnberg in 1539, is shown opposite.

We must now see what kind of music was available, and also

Ein außzug guter alter vñ new-
er Teutscher liedlein/einer rechten Teutschen art/
auff allerley Inſtrumenten zubrauchen/außerleſen.

Mein art vnd weiß in mittel maß
Gen andern ſtimmen iſt mein ſtraß
Die habent acht auff meine ſtim
Den Mennern ich für andern ſtim.

Tenor.

Getruckt zu Nürnberg bey Johan
Petreio anno M.D.XXXIX.

XXXVI. H. Iſaac.

Shruck ich muß dich laſſen/ich far do hin mein ſtraſſen/in fremde läd do

hin/mein freud iſt mir genomen/die ich nit weiß bekummē/wo ich jm e   lend

bin/ wo ich im e   lend bin.

who were the most important composers. Without exception, the composers were expert in singing and in the directing of choirs, so that whatever they composed was practicable. The aim of the sixteenth-century German composer was first to make sure that school (and church) choirs had material that was not too difficult, so that they could acquire a good working technique. But having developed good choirs—and taking into account the more professional groups of singers active in the Courts and in the larger city churches—endless possibilities existed of extending the range of choral music.

In general, there were three guide lines for the composer: the chorale, the Passion story, the secular song in parts.

Chorale melodies were in some cases adaptations of Gregorian hymns that had become popular. One of these was the familiar Whitsunday *Komm, heiliger Geist* (*Come, Holy Ghost*). Another, with German words replacing the original Latin, was the Eastertide *Christus ist erstanden* (*Christ is risen*), a tune which Luther loved and which was sung regularly by the audiences at the Easter Plays. Other tunes were adaptations of folk or popular songs. Of these the most famous, perhaps, was the song *Innsbruck ich muss dich lassen* (*I must leave Innsbruck*). This commemorates the composer's love of the Austrian city of Innsbruck where he used to stay as composer to the Emperor Maximilian I, but the song became known to the world as the "Passion Chorale". The melody was placed by Heinrich Isaac in the tenor part as is shown in the illustration on p. 71. Taken from the 1539 book published in Nürnberg, this shows how singers had to manage without the help of bar lines. As a chorale, this melody was often used, in one form or another, by composers, including J. S. Bach, in music for the liturgy of Passiontide.

Throughout the sixteenth century composers made arrangements of the chorales. Since they were well experienced in the style of music represented by the motet, they arranged the chorales in polyphonic manner, with an interesting line of melody for each part. At the same time they kept within practical limits. The aim which the Lutheran composers had in mind is expressed in the title of a collection issued by Georg Rhau in 1544: "New German Spiritual Songs, arranged in parts by various composers for use in the general schools". This collection contains a particularly fine setting of *Ein feste Burg* by Martin Agricola, who was the Cantor in the Cathedral School in Magdeburg.

Meanwhile, composers continued to write motets, but to German texts from the Lutheran Bible, and before long the themes of chorales were used as a basis for motet composition. This union of two traditions became one of the foundations on which the great works of the seventeenth and eighteenth centuries were built.

For some time the story of the Passion was set to music in two ways. First, in plainsong manner with a single melodic line. Second, in motet style, with the text set in parts throughout. There are examples of Latin Passions with a German translation written over the words. After the Reformation, Johann Walther composed a setting of the German text of the Passion in plainsong style—with brief choral interludes for the crowd scenes. This kind of Passion, with each character assigned to an appropriate voice, was more or less dramatic. There was, however, another style of Passion setting much in vogue, which consisted of the setting of the text, as in a motet, for a number of

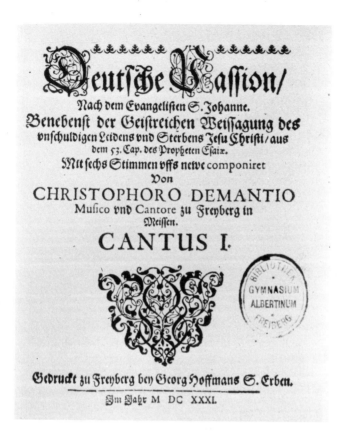

voices. The most popular motet-Passion was that composed by
Jakob Obrecht. Obrecht's Passion remained in favour until the
end of the sixteenth century.

Acknowledging the popularity of Obrecht's *Passion* Joachim
à Burgk (d. 1616) of Mühlhausen, issued a similar work in
1568, to the Luther text from St. John's Gospel. In his Introduction to this work, the composer said that it was written to
be sung and listened to in schools and churches. Other composers followed the example of à Burgk, and in 1631 Christoph
Demantius (1567–1643), Cantor in Freiberg, issued one of the
last of this kind of Passion (see illustrations p. 74 and above).

The style of music that was popular among the rank and file choirs in Germany during the sixteenth and into the seventeenth century, was on the whole conservative, resembling that of the Flemish and Italian masters in so far as harmony and sonorities were concerned. The distinguishing factors were the introduction of chorale *motiv* into motet design and the expressive qualities that came through an appreciation of the shape and implications of language.

But musical style is never static, and there were forces at work which gave a shake-up to attitudes to musical composition in Germany. During that entire period the rulers of the German States made strenuous efforts to improve their cultural standards, by studying developments in every branch of learning and art in other lands. So far as drama was concerned, there was a growing appreciation of the skill of English actors, and, towards the end of the sixteenth century, a number of English companies were engaged to play in German Courts and in the cities. These actors brought with them copies of English music, so that German societies became in due course enthusiastic singers of the principal English masters' madrigals.

But the principal inspiration for vocal music came from Italy. Before the sixteenth century was over, Italian musicians were engaged as members of the Court music in Dresden, while the Elector of Saxony was also arranging for promising young German musicians to study in Italy. Other rulers followed suit, so that, before long, the Italian style began to have a strong effect on that of German music.

The music in St. Mark's Cathedral, Venice, under the direction of the Gabrielis, was famous for its grandeur, its spaciousness, its variety of effects. The building was ideal for splitting the singers into groups, who were positioned at some distance from one another. With two- and three-choir music the listener had the impression of being surrounded with music. Since instrumental music was highly developed, the choral singing was accompanied by wind and stringed instruments which added

[76]

their own sonorities to the ensemble. At the same time, a higher degree of expressiveness was attained through an extension of chromatic harmony.

Hans Leo Hassler (1564–1612) was sent by the city of Nürnberg to study with Andrea Gabrieli. When he came back, he published a set of part songs described as "New German Songs in the style of Italian Madrigals and Canzonets". Hassler, who also composed many motets and chorales, worked in Nürnberg, Augsburg, Kassel, and Dresden. One of his most famous chorale settings is shown in the next example, the melody of which was frequently used at a later date by J. S. Bach. Notice the richness of the texture—there are two tenor parts to strengthen the middle register—and the flexible rhythm. This contrasts strongly with the form in which it is to be met in a modern hymnbook, where the rhythm is flattened out, making it much less effective (Ex. 9.)

EX. 9

Melchior Franck (1572–1639), a pupil of Hassler, was engaged by the Duke of Coburg to bring the music of his Court up to date. A master in many fields, Franck spent thirty years at Coburg and made an important contribution to the development of German music, especially in popularizing folk songs (of which he made arrangements in a number of collections) and in the provision of instrumental pieces.

The history of music is conveniently marked out for the student by the names of "great men". This is fair enough if it is realized that great men only existed as such because they were able to build on the work of many predecessors, and to take advantage of what their own environment offered. The great creative artists of the world summarize the attitudes of an era.

At the same time they interpret these attitudes. Often, in order to achieve their ideals (and ideals play an important part in the life of a genius), great artists need to display rare qualities of determination and endurance.

The greatest of German musicians of the seventeenth century was Heinrich Schütz (1585–1672). Born in Saxony, the son of a lawyer, Schütz was a choirboy in the Margraf's Chapel at Kassel. There he was taught by a fellow Saxon, George Otto (about 1544–1617), who, in turn, had been a pupil of Johann Walther—so we see the strong line of Lutheran tradition.

After studying law in the University of Marburg Schütz went to Venice, at the expense of the Margraf of Hesse. When he came back he was appointed to succeed Otto at Kassel. From there he went to the Electoral Chapel at Dresden, where he had the *Kreuzchor* and a distinguished group of solo singers and instrumentalists at his disposal. Schütz had already shown how deeply affected he was by the rich expressive style of Italian music for voices in the volume of madrigals which he had published in 1611. In 1619, he brought a new impulse into German church music with his *Psalms of David*. Here the old German motet style was enriched according to the more varied Italian manner. This gave scope for instrumental music, for a more vivid vocal style in which dramatic gestures and florid passage work were prominent, and for the exploitation of the contrasts afforded by independent voices and groups of voices.

At this stage, a term came into use to describe the new kind of music: "sacred symphony", or "sacred concerto". Another great master of this form was Samuel Scheidt (1587–1654), Kapellmeister to the Elector of Brandenburg and organist of the Church of Our Lady, in Halle. This was the town in which, thirty years after Scheidt's death, Handel was born.

The new style of church music had hardly taken effect in Germany before the country was plunged into the misery of one of the most disastrous and long-drawn-out wars in European history: the Thirty Years War (1618–48). During this war—between the Catholic forces of the Emperor and the Protestant powers of Europe—Germany was invaded many times, towns were destroyed, the countryside laid waste, the population savagely reduced by acts of war, and even more by famine and disease. Some musicians became refugees. Schütz was among them and he left Dresden (where he returned at the end of the war) to work at the Danish Court in Copenhagen, and at other Courts. But many musicians remained at their posts and, to their great credit, musical standards were somehow maintained. The choirs of the towns were, indeed, great aids to morale.

When the Thirty Years War finally came to an end Germany had been somewhat left behind in respect of the newer tendencies in music. Italy had forged ahead by the inauguration and development of opera, and it was not until the end of the seventeenth century that Germany began to exert an influence in this field. But the works of Heinrich Schütz were in themselves so monumental and so inspiring that most German composers were content to continue from where he had left off.

Schütz composed madrigals, motets, sacred symphonies, and concertos, settings of psalms, oratorio-type works for Easter and Christmas, four settings of the Passion, the "Seven last words from the Cross", as well as an opera and a ballet. Much of his music is published, but many manuscripts were lost when the City of Dresden was bombarded by the Prussian army in 1760. Schütz used voices and instruments with great originality and power, and expressed himself with dramatic force. It is, perhaps, not surprising in view of the troubled age in which he lived that his music often expresses a tragic mood.

The greatest of tragedies to the Christian was the Crucifixion. The Passion already had a long history in Germany. Schütz was a central figure in the history of Passion music, and his influence carried forward beyond the seventeenth century until it reached its climax in the works of J. S. Bach.

But Passion music was only one aspect of the revival of

music that took place in Germany in the second half of the seventeenth century. Composers in many towns and villages were active. They wrote many noble motets, often for two choirs, or for one four-part choir in conjunction with a unison group (of boys) to whom was entrusted the chorale that was so often introduced into the motet. They also crossed the motet style with that of the "sacred concerto", and the result was a "church cantata". In a church cantata, the central feature was the chorale, often broken down and treated in variation form, around which were placed instrumental interludes and passages for solo voices.

EX. 10

Among the important composers at the end of the century were several members of the Bach family, particularly Johann (1604–73), Heinrich (1615–92), Johann Christoph (1642–1703) and Johann Michael (1648–94). These men were influential figures in the development of music in Thuringia. Meanwhile, in Leipzig the Choir of St. Thomas's Church was being brought to a high level of perfection by its cantors. Of these outstanding were Sebastian Knüpfer (1633–?) and Johann Schelle (1648–1710), composers of church cantatas and of Passion music.

Georg Friedrich Händel was born not far from Leipzig and in his youth he heard much of the music that was performed there. It is tempting to believe that he heard, and remembered, a fine cantata-type setting of Psalm 26 by a forgotten composer of the Leipzig school. The same words that are set by Handel in *Messiah* in the chorus "Lift up your heads" occur in Knüpfer's setting (for five-part choir, two cornets, three trombones, strings, and organ). And both composers treat the question "Who is the King of Glory?" in almost the same way. This is the essence of the earlier setting of these words (Ex. 10).

There is another work of this period which is of interest in a Handelian connection: a motet by an unknown composer to the text "Glory to God in the highest, and peace on earth". The composer shows a straight line of melody (in the top part) to

EX. 11

suggest "peace on earth". Handel, although writing only in octaves (with no chords in the texture) has the same idea. The preceding passage, from the anonymous motet, shows this, and also the manner in which composers of that time liked to write for double choir (Ex. 11).

5

"Sing a Merry Madrigal"

MADRIGAL is a pretty word, and it sticks in the memory. Much more than part song, which is what a madrigal is. But it is a particular kind of part song. A madrigal is a setting of a secular poem. It is usually in three, four, five or six parts (with a preference for five parts). The style, in general, is imitative, with one voice imitating another, exactly as in the excerpt from Anerio's Mass on p. 62. The madrigal flourished during the ninety-year-period between the publication of a set of *Madrigali novi de diversi excellentissimi musici* (*New Madrigals by a number of very fine musicians*) in Rome, in 1533, and that of the *Songs in three, four, five and six parts*, of the English composer, Thomas Tomkins (about 1573–1656), in 1622.

In the field of secular music the madrigal now comes second to the folk song in the list of items necessary in a musical education to provide a foundation of "good taste". Since folk song, however, has been popularized in the modern sense (and in a contemporary, "beat"-conscious manner), the madrigal may have gone to the top of the list.

For this, there are a number of reasons. In Britain the idea that madrigals of British composition were once world-beaters is an attractive one. This is especially true of those who believe that the best music belonged to the past, and of those who consider that the Elizabethan age was the time in which Britons in all directions were at the top of their form. None of us are quite immune from the deception of self-flattery. Thus music in all countries is periodically paraded to bolster some show of national or, more aggressively, nationalist, pride.

The madrigal had its origins in folk song arrangements, and in secular part singing in general. The techniques of the secular part song, however, were refined by a reconsideration of the relationship between poetry and music. The most famous poet of the Italian Renaissance was Petrarch (1304–74) and his love poems were the inspiration of poets all over Europe for at least two centuries. Poets who wrote with the intention of having their poems set to music—and most did, at least occasionally—learned how to refine their styles in such a way that their ideas could be conveyed through the medium of music. The poetry which sixteenth-century composers most often set to music was simple in idea and precise in expression. It contained words and phrases that lent themselves to musical imitation, as is shown in the manner in which John Wilbye chooses his notes to illustrate the words "swell so high" on p. 97. It also expressed feelings, although often in a highly artificial manner. The notion that young people were prepared to "die for love" was generally approved, even though no one took it seriously.

The Flemish composers who flocked to Italy in large numbers during the sixteenth century brought together the techniques and styles of popular part song and motet, and produced a distinctive madrigalian pattern. This was more sophisticated than the part song, as it had existed, and lighter in movement than the motet. Willaert, Cyprien de Rore, Lassus, established the pattern, and while they were doing so Italian composers caught up with them in this exercise. Palestrina composed madrigals, but more famous in this respect were Orazio Vecchi (1550–1605), Luca Marenzio (about 1553–99), Giovanni Croce (about 1557–1609), Giovanni Gastoldi (who died about 1622), Carlo Gesualdo (about 1560–1615) and Claudio Monteverdi (1567–1643).

These composers were all, in one way or another, connected with church music, but moving in circles in which secular culture was increasingly more important than that of the church, they had every encouragement to compose madrigals. Madrigals were cultivated by the aristocracy, who took part in their performance, or engaged singers for the purpose. Sometimes professional singers were hired to fill in missing voices, and sometimes household servants were called in to assist. Madrigal poetry spread over a wide range of subjects and in consequence there was a variety of types of music. The main type—on the general theme of love—is described above, but on one hand the qualities of country life stimulated the descriptive gifts of composers such as Vecchi, and the impulse of the dance inspired the *Ballets* (a term used to indicate madrigal-type words of a lighter character) of Gastoldi. The influence of drama helped sometimes to bring the madrigal in the direction of tragedy or comedy. The madrigals of Gesualdo and Monteverdi are remarkable for their deep feelings, and for the increasing use of chromatic harmony to illustrate profounder emotions. The most popular of the Italian madrigalists, however, was Marenzio, and his was the pattern that was most emulated in other countries.

During the sixteenth and seventeenth centuries, every rich man in Europe made it his duty to visit Italy in order to pass himself off as cultured. Some poor scholars—like John Milton —also went to Italy. Musicians either made great sacrifices to go there, or persuaded a wealthy patron to subsidize a trip. In all cases, these seekers after culture came back with sets of madrigals which are still to be found in libraries in practically every European country. Sets of madrigals published in the sixteenth century are also to be found in the United States, obtained by later generations of culture-seekers!

Madrigals made a particularly strong impression in England. There the time was ripe for such a development. It was an age that was prolific in poetry. There was a long tradition of part singing. Wealth was spread over a broader section of the community than in most parts of Europe. Not only the aristocratic, ruling class was well off, but so, comparatively speaking, were many of the country landowners and the merchants of the towns. The Reformation had left the musical structure of the English church more or less as it had been before. Excellent trained musicians were in the employ of the greater churches to direct the professional choirs (of boys and men) that were the foundation of English musical culture. And, as elsewhere, there was a strong secular influence at work in society.

Although copies of Flemish and Italian madrigals, and French chansons, had been trickling into the country for a long time, it was not until the last twenty years of the sixteenth century that the trickle became a flood. Italian madrigals were translated into English, and then English composers, seeing a new opening for their talents, got to work.

It is hardly ever safe to say that one man is responsible for this or that. If, however, one were to propose a vote of thanks to anyone in particular for popularizing the madrigal cult in England it would be Nicholas Yonge (d. 1619), a "singing-man" of St. Paul's Cathedral, London.

Yonge was a man of enterprise. He entertained "a great number of Gentlemen and Merchants of good accompt (as well of this realme as of forreine nations)" at his house in the middle of London for the purpose of singing "Italian Songs, [which] are for sweetness of Aire, verie well liked of all, but most in account with them that understand that language". At this point Yonge wrote: "As for the rest, they doe either not sing them at all, or at the least with little delight." Yonge imported madrigal books from Italy regularly, and he managed to get hold of translations of a number of madrigals. He decided to publish a set of madrigals, including one by the English composer, William Byrd (1543–1623). He could hardly do otherwise, since Byrd held a monopoly in music publishing from Queen Elizabeth I. The first volume of madrigals to be

❧ Aegloga quarta.

ARGVMENT.

THis Aeglogue is purposely intended to the honor & praise of our most gratious Soueraigne, Queene *Elizabeth*. The speakers heereof be *Hobbinoll* and *Thenot*, two shepheards: the which *Hobbinoll* beeing before mentioned, greatly to haue loued *Colin*, is heere set forth more largely, complaining him of that boyes great misaduenture in loue, whereby his mind was alienated, and withdrawne not onely from him, who most loued him, but also from all former delights and studies, as well in pleasant piping, as cunning ryming and singing, and other his laudable exercises. Whereby hee taketh occasion, for proofe of his more excellencie and skill in poetrie, to record a song, which the said *Colin* sometime made in honour of her Maiestie, whom abruptly he tearmeth *Elisa*.

THENOT.

TEll me good HOBBINOL, what gars thee greet?
What? hath some Wolfe thy tender Lambs ytorne?
Or is thy Bagpipe broke, that sounds so sweet?
Or art thou of thy loued Lasse forlorne?

Or beene thine eyes attempred to the yeere,
Quenching the gasping furrowes thirst with raine?
Like Aprill showre, so streames the trickling teares
Adowne thy cheeke, to quench thy thirstie paine.

HOBBINOLL.

Nor this, nor that, so much doth make me mourne,
But for the lad, whom long I loued so deere,
Now loues a Lasse, that all his loue doth scorne:
He plung'd in paine, his tressed lockes doth teare.

HOBBINOLL.

Shepheards delights hee doth them all forsweare.
His pleasant Pipe, which made vs merriment,
He wilfully hath broke, and doth forbeare
His wonted songs, wherein he all out-went.

THENOT.

What is he for a Lad, you so lament?
Is loue such pinching paine, to them that proue?
And hath he skill to make so excellent,
Yet hath so little skill to bridle loue?

HOBBINOLL.

COLIN thou kenst the Southerne shepheards boy:
Him loue hath wounded with a deadly dart.
Whilome on him was all my care and ioy,
Forcing with gifts to winne his wanton hart.

But

published in England, therefore, was *Musica Transalpina*, collected by Nicholas Yonge, and dedicated to Lord Gilbert Talbot, heir to the Earldom of Shrewsbury. This was in 1588. The reasons for this publication were stated in his prefatory Dedication by Yonge, and it is from this document that the previous quotations are taken.

Also on the staff of St. Paul's Cathedral with Yonge was Thomas Morley (1558–1603). Morley was a fine composer, and, being greatly interested in Italian music, took the hint from Yonge and plunged into madrigalian composition. In 1593, he published a set of three-part songs (called *Canzonets*), which followed an established English preference for part songs in three parts but which had the wit and elegance of Italian style. Two years later, he issued the first book in England to use the word madrigal. His *Madrigalls to Four Voyces* contained one of the most popular of English compositions of this kind— "Aprill is in my Mistris face". In 1595 came a set of *Balletts to Five Voyces*, in which is to be found "Now is the month of Maying". In the same year a collection unique in English music appeared—a book of *Canzonets to two Voices*. Morley's next publication showed how keen the English still were to sing the masterpieces of Italian part song. *Canzonets or little short songs to Foure voyces: selected out of the best and approved Italian Authors* was dedicated not to an aristocratic personage but to "Maister Henrie Tapsfield, Citizen and Grocer of the Citie of London". It contains pieces by Giovanni Bassano (who had relatives in London), Croce, Felice Anerio (about 1560–1614; brother of Giovanni Francesco), Viadana (whose real name was Lodovico Grossi, about 1564–1645), Vecchi, and Morley himself. In the same year Morley published his own set of *Aers to five and sixe Voices*, while in 1601 he made another anthology and issued madrigalian works by twenty-three of the leading English composers as a tribute to Queen Elizabeth. This was *The Triumphes of Oriana*, at the end of each of which stood the loyal refrain: "Long live fair Oriana."

[88]

Among the composers represented in this collection were John Bennet (about 1570 to about 1620), Michael Cavendish (about 1565–1682), Michael East (about 1580–1648), John Farmer (sixteenth to seventeenth century), Robert Jones (d. about 1617), John Milton (about 1563–1647), Richard Nicholson (d. 1639), Daniel Norcome (1576 to about 1626), Thomas Weelkes (about 1575–1623), and John Wilbye (1574–1638), as well as Morley himself. Distinguished composers who, for some reason or other, did not contribute were William Byrd and Orlando Gibbons (1583–1625). These composers represent a cross section of musical life, and of Elizabethan–Jacobean society. The fact that they were by no means all practising in London indicates a general interest in madrigal performance. There is additional evidence of this in the dedications of collections other than *The Triumphes of Oriana*.

Bennet lived in Cheshire. Robert Jones was a Welshman. East was organist of Lichfield Cathedral; Farmer, of Christ Church Cathedral, Dublin; Nicholson, of Magdalen College, Oxford University; Weelkes, of Chichester Cathedral. Michael Cavendish belonged to a landowning family in Suffolk. Milton, father of the poet, worked in London, where he was a clerk. Wilbye was resident musician to a wealthy family in Suffolk. William Byrd and Orlando Gibbons were Court musicians, who exercised great influence on the musical life of London in many different ways.

Since the madrigal had its origins in a keen interest in poetry and its relation to music, and since England was well stocked with poets during the period under discussion, it is not surprising to find the names of some of the great poets among the authors of the words of the madrigals. (Many texts of madrigals, however, were not ascribed to particular poets.) Edmund Spenser, Philip Sidney, Christopher Marlowe, Nicholas Breton, Thomas Campion (also a composer), and Walter Raleigh, all appear as composers of madrigal verses. In general the texts were of a pastoral nature, and many madrigals provide delicious and evocative pictures of country life. Among these are Morley's "Now is the month of Maying", Weelkes's "Lo! country sports", Wilbye's "Sweet, honey-sucking bees". Since love is a perennial topic in poetry, it is not surprising that it is strongly featured in madrigalian verse. Usually idealized and described according to literary convention as existing between shepherds and shepherdesses. They were not real life shepherds and shepherdesses, however, but those whose only dwelling-place was the legendary Arcadia.

Sometimes the Arcadian and the real worlds meet. Queen Elizabeth often made tours (they were called "progresses") and whenever she did so, entertainments were devised. Always there were fairies (the best-looking girls of the area dressed up) and in pretty verses Elizabeth (or *Oriana*) was greeted as the Fairy Queen. This kind of scene is shown in the illustration from Spenser's *Shepheardes Calendar* shown on p. 87. It is described many times in *The Triumphes of Oriana*, but nowhere more enchantingly than in Daniel Norcome's contribution to that collection. Here are the original words:

> With Angels face and brightnesse
>   And orient hew
> faire *Oriana* shining,
> with nimble foote she tripped,
> O're hils, and mountaines,
> at last in dale she rested:
> this is that maiden *Queene* of the Fayrie land,
> with scepter in hir hand.
> the Faunes and Satires dauncing,
> did show their nimble lightness.
> Faire *Nais* came,
> the Nimphes did leave their bowers,
> & brought their baskets full of hearbes & flowers.
> Then sang the shepherds and Nymphs of *Diana*,
> Long live faire *Oriana*.

But the texts of madrigals were not limited. There were some poems of a philosophical nature, that particularly attracted Byrd and Gibbons. Madrigals of the character of "Retire, my soul", by Byrd, and "What is our life?" by Gibbons, come very near to being anthems (the anthem being the British counterpart to the continental motet).

One of the best loved of all English madrigals is "The Silver Swan"—a popular myth already immortalized in "October" in the *Shepheardes Calendar*—by Orlando Gibbons. This is distinguished by a very beautiful melody in the top part, to which the lower voices—while still making points of imitation —provide what seems to be much more like an accompaniment. This represents a change of attitude on the part of composers and their patrons. From the beginning of the seventeenth century the old contrapuntal style, which had persisted for so long, was becoming less popular. The preference now was for melody, supported by discreet chordal accompaniments, by strings or, more particularly, by lute or keyboard instrument. The English madrigal, partly under pressure from Italy, partly from a natural acclimatization to popular use, developed a simpler texture, and a new term came in. The part song of the early seventeenth century was described as an "Ayre" (see Morley p. 95).

The greatest of British composers of Ayres was John Dowland (1563–1626), who was born in Dublin but (for religious reasons) spent much of his life in Europe. He was employed at different times at the Courts of Brunswick, Hesse and Copenhagen, and published music in France, Holland, and Germany. Some of Dowland's Ayres were composed as part songs (with the possibility of entrusting the lower parts to instruments), others as solo songs with instrumental accompaniment. Among the part songs are "Now, O now I needs must part" and "Come away, sweet love", which have retained their popularity across the centuries.

Although originally, English madrigals owed a good deal in the first place to the example of the Flemish and Italian musicians of the sixteenth century, they developed their own distinctive character. For the first time since the days of John Dunstable, English music, through the madrigal (and, to some extent, through keyboard and string music) broke into the European market. The Margraf Moritz of Hesse, who was the patron of Heinrich Schütz, also employed John Dowland. Moreover, he possessed works by Thomas Weelkes, Thomas Campion and Philip Rosseter (about 1575–1623), who collaborated with Campion in the issue of a joint book of Ayres. The madrigals and ballets of Morley were published in Germany, with the texts translated into German.

Songs and part songs which belonged to the repertoire of the touring English actors were also published in Germany, together with the texts of their plays. And in Dresden particularly, at the beginning of the seventeenth century, madrigals from England were used by the *Kantoreien*.

In the twentieth century, there has been a notable revival of interest in madrigal singing, both among amateurs and professionals, and English madrigals are prominent in the general repertoire. Once again they are being published in Europe to meet an ever-increasing demand, and there are brilliant recordings of some of the finest examples by German, Rumanian, and Czech madrigal groups. The famous Rumanian Madrigal Choir is shown in the next illustration. The perfection of some modern performances, however, tends to hide something of the original function of the madrigal, and even more, the kinds of performance that we might have heard when such music was new.

When music from former times is revived, it is often given under conditions originally unknown, which make for a quality of execution that the composers could only have dreamed of. There is no reason to complain of this, but the point should be borne in mind. What we regard as a perfect performance of old music includes ideas—about interpretation especially—that were not familiar to the composers of such music, and leaves

[92]

out other ideas that were. This is inevitable, even though scholars try to produce editions that are free from later notions of expression, simply because musical notation is only capable of showing the bare outlines of music.

In the Renaissance and immediate post-Renaissance periods, writers often idealized the art of music. But there was no idea that works should do more than serve for the society or occasion for which they were written. In an exciting, zestful age when almost every practising musician was a composer, there was a constant desire for change. The madrigal thus gave way to the Ayre, the part song to the solo song. But the cult of the madrigal had established the social practice of singing together. Because musical fashion had changed, those who had become accustomed to enjoying themselves in performing madrigals saw no reason to discontinue their custom. The madrigal began its career as an embellishment of aristocratic life. By the time its form had given way to others, it was happily fixed in the affections of the middle classes.

That the madrigal has been idealized is not entirely the fault of enthusiasts of today. If we tend to think of England in the sixteenth century as a country in which everybody sang complicated part songs, and in which the amateur whose capacity for sight reading was beyond reproach, the reason partly lies in the enthusiastic authors of those times. Among them were many who would have been a boon to the modern public-relations industry.

Writing in 1579, before the madrigal in fact had got under way, Edmund Spenser described his shepherds of the *Shepheardes Calendar* as expert in "pleasant piping", and in "cunning riming and singing". In the section that deals with the month of April one shepherd—Colin—anticipates *The Triumphes of Oriana* by making a song "in honour of her Majesty, whom abruptly he tearmeth *Elisa*". The anonymous artist who added a woodcut to the head of the 1619 edition showed a nice company of rural musicians giving a performance before Her Majesty. Sometimes, to be truthful, such performances were given before the Queen—but not usually by untrained agricultural workers and their wives and sweethearts.

Thomas Morley (as well as others) built up the illusion of a universal enthusiasm for cultured singing. So in one madrigal the words read:

> Now is the gentle season freshly flowring,
> to sing and play and daunce while May endureth,
> and wooe & wed toe [=too], that sweet delight procureth.

Morley—whose most famous part song leads us to think of May as a month specially dedicated to madrigal singing—was a first-class propagandist. In 1597 he wrote a celebrated textbook on the theory and practice of music—*A Plain and Easie Introduction to Practicalle Musicke*. The title of the first part of this book is "Teaching to Sing". A young man, Philomathes, goes out to a party:

> But supper being ended and music books (according to the custom) being brought to the table, the mistress of the house presented me with a part earnestly requesting me to sing; but when, after many excuses, I protested unfeignedly that I could not, every one began to wonder; yea, some whispered to others demanding how I was brought up. . . .

The young man, therefore, decided to waste no time and went to a master to teach him the art of singing, so that he could no longer be an object of ridicule in society. Morley's technique was precisely that of a modern advertising agent. He was out to sell music—not least because he himself had music to sell. The best way to do it was to suggest that the musically incompetent were undesirable members of polite society and out of the fashion.

Philomathes duly went for instruction, which is very thoroughly laid out in "Teaching to Sing", where there were many useful sight-reading exercises. These are of increasing difficulty and conclude with a number of two-part examples. About these the music master says:

> Here be some following of two parts which I have made of purpose, that when you have any friend to sing with you, you may practise together, which will sooner make you perfect than if you should study never so much by yourself.

Good advice!

Here we see the beginning of one of Morley's two-part exercises, which if you have a friend (as Morley suggested) you may

For
2 voices

EX. 12

try to sing. The two parts are closely related, the thematic openings being transferred from the one to the other in the imaginative manner that has already been noticed (compare p. 83). At the point where *x x* occurs, the music changes its tonal centre. Actually since it moves clearly from the key of F major to C major it strikes us as being modern. What it illustrates is that the modal system was approaching its end.

But the modal flavour was still strong, as is shown in the next example, from the three-part madrigal, *Weepe O mine eies*, by John Wilbye. The common chords marked *x* are arrived at because of the movement of the individual parts according to the principles of modal behaviour even though this is slightly modified. This example also shows the beautiful rhythmic flexibility that was characteristic of the madrigal. The final section quite clearly is in three-time. Those who first sang this music needed to be quick in the uptake. Wilbye (and his contemporaries) simply set down the exact note lengths, prefaced by a time signature. They did not mark changes of time, because such changes were thought of as variations written over the basic pattern of the piece. Often such variations did not coincide in all the parts (Ex. 13).

EX. 13

This is quiet music, better to be understood from the inside than the outside. It was meant for singers rather than for audiences. Because of this it has a sense of intimacy and its own particular charm.

6

Cross Currents

FROM the historian's point of view, the seventeenth century is a period of endless fascination; it was also a period in which many of the patterns that have affected modern life and thought began to take shape. It was an age of powerful ideologies. These were still stated in religious terms, but increasingly they showed distinctive political and social viewpoints. The seventeenth century was the first great period of scientific discovery—in the sense that the work of scientists (in the broad meaning of the word) began to be recognized as affecting the lives of communities and the character of philosophy. Before the seventeenth century, the idea that kings (and hereditary rulers in general) were appointed by God was generally accepted. During the seventeenth century this idea was discredited. A period of change is a period of unrest. Between 1618 and 1648 one of the most devastating wars in European history, as has already been told, was waged. As a result of this the vitality of half of Europe, and virtually the whole of Germany, was grievously sapped. Yet after the disaster recovery was quick.

The age was one of antagonism between Protestant and Catholic States; of division of Protestantism into Calvinist and non-Calvinist; of increasing prosperity for some and of widespread poverty for others; of a growing belief in the saving grace of reasonable thought; and of a powerful and entrenched reliance on superstition.

Music, as always, was affected by the general atmosphere of change. In a broad sense, especially in the field of choral music, it became more aristocratic on the one hand, and more democratic on the other. In Italy, in particular, the music of the church expanded in every direction, taking advantage of, and adding to, the resources of secular music. There was not only the statutory music of the liturgy, but also music of religious character based on the pattern of the newly established opera. Against the overpowering magnificence—as it then seemed—of the music of the cathedrals of Rome, Venice, Bologna and so on, there was, however, the stark simplicity of the Genevan Psalm that was all the music permitted in the Reformed churches of France and Scotland, and of some parts of Germany. Between these two extremes stood the gradually evolving choral music of the Church of England and the Lutheran church in Germany and in some other parts of northern Europe. In Catholic church music the ordinary citizen took little or no part: he listened, often with admiration, but with no chance of affecting its character. In the music of the Reformed churches the ordinary citizen, with varying degrees of responsibility, did have some part to play.

An age of change is one in which traditions overlap. Old ones, though often under fire, continue, and new ones emerge. We have already mentioned the beginnings of opera in the seventeenth century. That these took place when and where they did was symptomatic of a whole range of interlinked new ideas.

The chief characteristic of music until the time of the High Renaissance (the end of the long process that began in the fourteenth century and altogether, and rather imprecisely, known as the Renaissance) was its polyphonic and contrapuntal character. Essentially this music was for voices. Even though voices were often supported by instruments, these merely doubled the vocal parts. The same kind of music served for religious and secular purposes, the distinction between motet and madrigal being a fine one.

Now the basis of music that is sung is the word, and the question of balance between music and word is one that always exercises—or should exercise—the mind of the composer (and also of the singer). Polyphonic music hardly gave the words a fair chance. In church music, where the texts were supposed to be familiar, this did not matter all that much. In relation to the words of lyrical poems it did matter. In the case of words of dramatic character, and intended for theatrical presentation, it mattered a good deal more.

In the late sixteenth and early seventeenth centuries poets, musicians, and interested and informed amateurs (for the most part aristocrats with plenty of time to spare), took a fresh look at the words–music relationship and came up with the proposition that polyphony should be regarded as out. Because conditions were more favourable there than anywhere else, the proposition was most energetically adopted in Italy. The "new music" as it was hopefully described began in Florence.

The consequences of the theory and practice of the leading Florentine musical reformers—Giovanni Bardi (1534–1612), Giulio Caccini (about 1545–1618) and Jacopo Peri (1561–1633), were the song for solo voice, accompanied by chords on the lute that would not get in the way of the vocal line. There were two kinds of song that developed. The one, in which the words were of primary importance, was sung to the rhythm of the words. Being, as it were, recited, this was called *recitative*. The other kind of song, in which the emotion within the text was intended to be conveyed through the vocal line, was called *aria*. This emphasis on the single voice led to a reconsideration of the art of singing, and, inevitably, to an enhancement of the status of the singer. As soon as the singer realized that his status had improved he expected the fact to be registered in the kind of music he was expected to sing.

Adding together the various influences that were brought to bear, certain facts emerged. Vocal music became more expressive. Recitative encouraged singers to develop a dramatic delivery. Through aria they learned to vary their dynamics, to make full use of the contrasts of *piano* and *forte*. Rhythms became less inflexible, because singers began to take liberties where they thought it desirable, and the *rubato* style was added to the emotional possibilities of musical expression. The first printed book of music to include terms of expression and indications of time was *Musiche Sacre e Morale* (1640), for one, two and three voices, by Domenico Mazzocchi (1592–1665).

At the same time, proud of their technical accomplishments and taking full advantage of their public appearances, singers developed the voice as an instrument, able to perform the most florid passages (similar to those played by violins) and intricate ornaments. Vocal music passed through the hands of Claudio Monteverdi (1567–1643), Pietro Cavalli (1602–76), Giacomo Carissimi (1605–74), Alessandro Scarlatti (1660–1725), Antonio Vivaldi (about 1675–1741), and through the throats of hundreds of Italian singers who became famous all over Europe. The techniques of singing were detailed in text-books. Of these one of the most famous was by Pier Francesco Tosi (1646–1727) and it was called (in English) *The Art of the Florid Song*, which gives some indication of the kind of singing expected. This book was first published, in Italian, in 1723, and was later issued in English and German editions.

During this period, not only did singers become more accomplished, but new types of singers became fashionable. Towards the end of the sixteenth century, men who could cover the high register of the boy's voice were imported from Spain into the Sistine Chapel Choir. These singers, by training their throat muscles, sang in a manner which (since they had normal tenor or bass voices otherwise) was described as *falsetto* (false). Such singers were and continued to be employed in English cathedrals for the alto part. They have come back into vogue in the twentieth century with the revival of old music and the general attempt to reproduce as nearly as possible the original conditions of performance. The *falsetto* tone was so much sought after in the seventeenth and eighteenth centuries that promising boy singers were sometimes made to undergo an operation known as castration which ensured that their voices would not "break". These singers were described as *castrati*, and many became rich and famous. Their tone was both brilliant and strong.

The emancipation of women has been a long and difficult process. Among the first women to enjoy some independence were those who were good singers. One of the earliest women singers to appear in public (at least in so far as singing at court may be described as public) was Francesca Caccini, daughter of Giulio (see p. 100). After her, during the seventeenth century, came a long line of opera and oratorio singers. A soprano voice added its own brilliance to music; the contralto voice (cultivated as such a little later) added warmth, or a sense of mystery—as you will. So far as choral music was concerned, however, women did not get much of a look in until well into the eighteenth century. In the early years of the eighteenth century Johann Mattheson had caused some eyebrow raising by introducing women singers into the cantata performances that were given in the Hamburg churches of which he was musical director. But this was exceptional. Even in 1763, when Thomas Arne, of London, had women singers for the chorus of his oratorio, *Judith*, he was thought to be very daring. The main body of church music was confined to choirs of boys and men —a hangover from the doctrines of the medieval church.

While so much was taking place in relation to singing, there was also a great and significant development on the side of instrumental music. At the beginning of the seventeenth century, purely instrumental music lagged behind vocal music. But by the beginning of the eighteenth century, when the terms *suite, sonata*, and *concerto* had aquired distinctive meanings to indicate forms of purely instrumental music, such music was leading an independent existence and we were within sight of the modern orchestra. Instruments and voices had long been

[102]

in partnership, but with the instrumental group the junior partner. Opera and oratorio, the dramatic forms into which music was guided, provided the instruments with a much more important role. In short, they, in their own way and with their own tonal associations, could add evocative detail to the description of sights and scenes contained in the words. And they could provide atmosphere.

Now, it must not be thought that voices and instruments were engaged in some kind of feud. Each had waited for suitable conditions under which to co-operate with the other. In the post-Renaissance period these conditions were present—to the great benefit of music and musicians. As has been seen vocal technique borrowed from instrumental, especially violin, technique. But composers of instrumental music also aimed to make instruments "sing".

In an age of change, traditions overlap. In the music of the Catholic church the style of Palestrina was, and continued to be, thought of as an ideal. Through all the changes brought about by fresh attitudes to technique and to taste the Masses and motets of this great master and of the greatest of his contemporaries, held their place. Apart from anything else there were in existence many choirs, expensively maintained, for whom there was no music better designed to show both their corporate skills. In addition to this, the music of the polyphonic composers had the reputation of possessing higher spiritual value than any other kind of music. This was partly a matter of the clarity of the style, partly a growing tendency to think that old music was in some way superior to modern. The strict polyphonic style was called the "old style", and composers continued to write in it—or in a style very little removed from it—when composing for the church.

Monteverdi, a key figure in the history of music, wrote Masses in the "old style", the last of which was not published until 1651, after his death. In this last Mass almost the only concession to modernity is the provision of a figured bass (a bass

[103]

with figures below, from which the keyboard player—in this case the organist—could work out appropriate harmonies). Otherwise it has the simplicity and austerity proper to the sixteenth-century style. But Monteverdi, one of the first great composers of opera, applied to other church music all the resources of harmonic variety, vocal virtuosity and instrumental variety that had become available.

The greatest of his works of this order is a set of movements collectively known as the *Vespers of the Virgin Mary*. In the following example, from the setting of Psalm 109 in the Vespers, there is a vivid contrast between the first chord, sounded six times, and the exciting movement of the voices and instruments that follows. This is far removed from the calm mood of the Palestrina style, and shows how dramatic ideas were being introduced (Ex. 14).

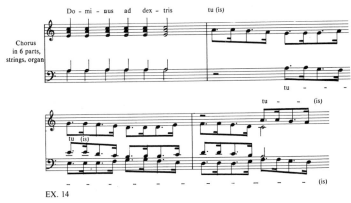

EX. 14

The co-existence of two styles, however, continued. In strictly liturgical music the polyphonic method was encouraged —not only in Catholic but also in much Protestant church music, particularly in England (where the works of the Eliza-bethan composers held their place in the services of the Church), and in Germany, where the contrapuntal prelude based on a chorale melody, for organ (a "Chorale Prelude"), was a strong influence on composers of choral music.

In the meantime, new musical forms crystallized. The song extended into the *cantata,* which consisted of a sequence of recitatives and arias, interspersed with instrumental pieces and with occasional duets and other ensemble vocal items and often with concluding choruses. An opera was always based on a secular story, usually taken from classical mythology. Side by side with opera, there grew up a religious counterpart; this was called oratorio (because it started in a Roman church called an oratory). Oratorio of the later seventeenth century was formally almost indistinguishable from opera, except that, with luck, there was more work for a chorus.

In many oratorios there was excellent dramatic reason for

EX. 15

the introduction of chorus, for by it the idea of a whole people (e.g. "The children of Israel") could be effectively represented.

One of the great pioneers of oratorio was the Roman composer, Giacomo Carissimi (1605–74), who brought together the "old" and the "new" styles, and who placed more importance on the chorus in his oratorios than most of his contemporaries. An excerpt from a *Magnificat*, for four solo and four chorus voices, shows the extent to which he was influenced by the dignity of the old Roman style. But above the long notes of the theme in the bass the trumpet-like shape of the *motiv* of the upper voices suggest a sense of brilliance and grandeur and an extension into music of the meaning of the word *magna* (great) (Ex. 15).

Carissimi's best-known oratorios were *Jonah* and *Jephtha*. From *Jephtha* Handel borrowed a chorus for his oratorio *Samson*.

The form of oratorio became increasingly popular in Italy (especially among the clergy for whom it was a convenient and attractive substitute for opera) and at the end of the seventeenth and the beginning of the eighteenth centuries the ecclesiastical market was flooded with works of this kind. Mostly they gave opportunity to solo singers to demonstrate their virtuoso skills and their powers of interpretation; choral numbers (except in the case of Carissimi) were usually only placed at the beginning and the end of acts. One energetic composer of oratorio was Antonio Draghi (1635–1700), whose thirty-seven works of this kind ranged from the allegorical *Eternity and Time* (1683) to the dramatics of what became a popular subject—*The Judgement of Solomon* (date uncertain). Draghi was highly esteemed in Vienna, where he was Court musician. Alessandro Scarlatti (1660–1725), a leading and versatile Neapolitan composer, was also highly respected in Vienna where his oratorio, *The Repentant Magdalene* was performed in 1693. A Viennese composer, Johann Georg Reutter (about 1708–72) took up the

oratorio tradition to good effect. Reutter, director of music in
St. Stephen's Cathedral, was the teacher of Josef and Michael
Haydn.

The spread of Italian music at this time was spectacular.
Opera was universal in its influence. Oratorio, for the time
being, was restricted to Roman Catholic countries. The contribution made by Italian composers in this respect has not,
perhaps, been fully appreciated in Protestant countries. Attilio

EX. 16

Ariosti (1666–?) a much-travelled composer, with whom
Handel became acquainted during his boyhood, made the story
of *Nebuchadnezzar* (much later the subject of an opera by
Verdi) into an oratorio. Antonio Caldara (1670–1736) was a

brilliant master of choral effect. The excerpt on p. 107 from a Magnificat (four solo voices, four chorus voices, oboe, strings, organ) shows the beginnings of a style in choral writing made familiar by the music of Handel. An exciting passage for soprano solo is set off by strong choral interjections (of "Amen"), but then the mobile character of the solo part is transferred to the chorus (Ex. 16).

This was composed some time before 1710—by which time Handel was an established composer who had lately spent three profitable years in Italy. It is not surprising that the style of Caldara reminds us of that of Handel. One of Caldara's oratorios—*The Death and Burial of Christ* was performed in 1724 in Salzburg, the birthplace of Mozart. In 1733, *St. Helen at Calvary*, by Leonard Leo (1694–1744) was given at Brno, in what is now Czechoslovakia. In the opening of this oratorio (Ex. 17), there is a new kind of choral expressiveness. The chromatic harmonics suggest the idea of suffering (*pena*) in such a way that they seem very nearly independent either of melody or rhythm, even though the imitative manner of the "old style" is still evident. This kind of harmonic expression was to be much exploited in choral music of later time. Similar passages occur in the choral music of Mozart and Haydn, both of whom were greatly influenced by Italian models.

We must now retrace our steps a little. Although Italian stylistic changes had a great effect on music generally they could only become fully effective when conditions were advantageous. Broadly speaking, this referred to periods when some people were prepared to invest large sums of money in music. When this was not the case the rate of change in music was somewhat slowed down. In England and Germany, in particular, there were other strong conservative factors to consider in connection with choral music. And both countries were disrupted by war and political turmoil in the middle of the seventeenth century.

The pattern of music in the German states was a complex

[instrumental parts omitted]

EX. 17

one, for their rulers, whenever possible, tried to carry forward
the progressive ideas that had begun to be absorbed at the
beginning of the century. Also, after the end of the Thirty
Years War there was a great revival of music-making. The
church choirs regained their former standing; the court music
establishments gained in strength, and there was a new and
lively interest in music in the universities. Because of the
political structure of the German states, all these developments
were interrelated. Music of the towns benefited from the
presence of Court Kapellmeisters, who were often glad to
co-opt the services of town musicians, and particularly musically trained schoolboys, at least for special court occasions.

[109]

The traditions of church music were maintained and the chorale retained its central function. The motet in which a chorale was placed as the central feature of the music—as a *cantus firmus*—gradually changed, and, by the end of the century, the particular form known as the church cantata was established. The church cantata—peculiar to Germany—was a sequence of recitatives and arias, interspersed with chorales. The literary form, in imitation of the pattern of the Italian cantata, or opera, was evolved by a Hamburg poet and clergyman, Erdmann Neumeister (1671–1756). Together with the church cantata, the traditional music for Passiontide went in the same direction. In both cases the choral element was strong.

Side by side with the church cantata was the secular cantata, which was an important part of any celebration—whether of a Duke's birthday, the inheritance of his estate by a landowner, the appointment of a university professor, or a royal visit to a city. Not far distant from this kind of cantata was the more dramatic entertainment of the *Singspiel*, a play with music rather than an opera in the Italian manner. The characteristics of the *Singspiel* were, a German text, a more or less topical subject, and a tendency to use popular songs—or songs in popular idiom—rather than the more elaborate type of Italian aria. What took place in German music, during the seventeenth century, culminated in the music of Johann Sebastian Bach, other members of the Bach family, as well as many other composers, in the eighteenth century. This will be considered in the next chapter.

Germany had its ruling dukes. England did not. For a brief period, it even lost its king as a result of the Civil War between Cavaliers and Roundheads from 1641 to 1652. This war was caused by the conviction of the commercial class that the government of the Stuarts, and particularly of Charles I, was not only incompetent but also corrupt. There were other factors, of course, but, in the main, the war symbolized a change in the relative power of the social classes. Aristocratic influence was lessened; middle-class influence increased. This was reflected in attitudes to the arts, and, in particular, towards music.

When Nicholas Yonge published *Musica Transalpina* he had principally in mind the kind of people who had for some time been coming to his home to sing. The great spate of madrigal production evidenced a wide spread of interest in this form of music. To sing a part in a madrigal requires a considerable degree of musical competence. The madrigal was simplified, as in the Ayre, which could be sung either by a group of singers, or by a solo voice with instrumental accompaniment. This simplification was brought about by a general trend towards monody (single line music) and away from polyphony—as in Italian music—and also by an increasing demand. This increasing demand was quickly appreciated by some musicians, and by none more than the London musician, Thomas Ravenscroft (about 1590 to about 1633).

In 1609, Ravenscroft published two sets of part songs—airs, catches, rounds, and so on, often traditional and from the realm of popular music. These were entitled *Pammelia* and *Deuteromelia*. In his Introduction to the former, Ravenscroft stated quite explicitly that the pieces were meant for those "whose love of music exceeds their skill", and that they were "pleasing without difficulty". In 1611, another collection, *Melismata*, appeared.

Some of the songs that Ravenscroft popularized, like "Three Blind Mice", passed into the repertoire of children's music and have remained there to the present day. Others were not suitable as children's music since the words were of an improper character. This, however, was no disqualification in the public houses of London (and other towns), and, although clergymen often raised voices of protest, such songs were a means of spreading an uninhibited love of vocal music. Other musicians followed Ravenscroft's lead and John Hilton (1599–1657) published *Ayres or Fa La's for Three Voyces* in 1627 and edited a set of pieces, described by their punning title, *Catch that Catch can*.

Groups met together informally to sing catches, as we know from Samuel Pepys's *Diary*. There were also less informal groups that began to constitute Clubs. One such Club was established in Dublin, Ireland, in 1679–80, by the singing men of the two Cathedrals, Christ Church and St. Patrick. This was the first Catch Club definitely to be recorded as such.

So we are brought back again to the subject of church music. In Britain this took two forms. On the one hand there was the continuing tradition of the anthem, on the other the metrical psalm. The latter, taken over from the Calvinists, was the English counterpart of the German chorale, and if it did not have anything like the same historical significance it was an important feature of worship. The metrical psalm was a psalm from the Bible put into simple verse form. By its side there developed the hymn, of which the words were more independent. When the metrical psalm was regularized in the sixteenth century, many fine melodies, primarily from the Genevan Psalter (of 1552) were popularized. These were the mainstay of congregational singing. From the sixteenth and through the seventeenth centuries many volumes of Psalms were published, a famous collection of the seventeenth century being Ravenscroft's *The Whole Booke of Psalmes, with the Hymnes Evangelicall, and Songs Spirituall*, etc. (1621).

In country places, the singing of the psalms often left much to be desired. There was no general and widespread system of musical education (such as had left its lasting influence in Germany) and congregations had to learn laboriously the tunes by heart. To this end, they were helped by the Precentor (in Scotland) or by the Parish Clerk (in England). The Precentor or the Clerk would sing one or two lines, as does a teacher in a school, and the congregation would follow his example as best they could. This practice was known as "lining out".

Psalm singing was popular because it was one of the few forms in which the poorer people could collectively express themselves in music. In Britain it was to become the founda-

[112]

tion of a great choral movement. The same is true of America. The first emigrants from Europe, in the seventeenth century, often left their countries on account of their religious convictions. Among the first collections of music to be taken across the Atlantic were volumes of Psalms, published in London. Among them were John Day's *The Whole Booke of Psalmes* (1562), a version of the first famous English Psalter issued by Thomas Sternhold (d. 1549) and John Hopkins (d. 1570), which was used by the Puritans who settled around Boston before 1630; Richard Allison's *Psalmes of David* (1599), a copy of which was found among the belongings of William Brewster, who died in Plymouth (Mass.) in 1643; and Ravenscroft's Psalter, of which Governor John Endecott owned a copy. In 1640, an American Psalter, *The Whole Booke of Psalms Faithfully Translated into English Metre*, was published in Cambridge, Mass. This first American Psalter was popularly known as the *Bay Psalm Book*, and it ran into many editions. No tunes, however, were printed with the words, and its users were referred for the melodies to Ravenscroft's collection. Life in America during the seventeenth century was hard; and music did not rank high on the list of priorities. So it is not surprising that, by the beginning of the eighteenth century, there were many complaints about the indifferent and incorrect singing in churches.

"For want of exactitude," said one writer in 1721, "I have observed in many places one man is upon a note, while another a note behind, which produces something hideous and beyond expression bad." In that same year of 1721, the Rev. John Tufts, of Boston, began to establish some kind of foundation on which a popular musical education might be based. In short, he established procedures for the development of competence in sight reading. (See illustration p. 114.)

Just as ability to read the printed word increased man's knowledge of the world, so the power to read music widened his interest in that art. It also affected the character of music.

[113]

In England the greatest musical figure of the late seventeenth century, and one of the masters of all times, was Henry Purcell (1658–95). Expert in all branches of music he was, above all, one of the supreme masters of vocal music, and he did more than any previous composer in England to develop the art of choral music. Purcell, who learned to sing the Elizabethan–Jacobean masterpieces of English church music as a chorister in the Chapel Royal, wrote anthems after this manner, but

[114]

introduced daring harmonies of great originality. Some of his anthems, however, showed the influence of the cantata method of the Italians and of the clear and rhythmic style of the French. French influence was especially strong, since Charles II had spent his years of exile at the Court of Louis XIV, and Purcell was able to employ a fine string orchestra similar to one established in Paris by Jean Baptiste Lully (1632–87).

Purcell's most ambitious work for church use was his setting of the *Te Deum and Jubilate* in D, which was composed for the opening of St. Paul's Cathedral in 1694. This work, for a larger choir than was usual and for orchestra, created a great sensation. More works of similar nature were written, notably by Dr. William Croft (1678–1717), and by Handel. Handel's *Utrecht Te Deum* (1713) was a link between the traditional English anthem and the later English oratorio.

Purcell composed Odes (cantatas, but with important choral movements) for St. Cecilia's Day (November 22), for royal and various secular occasions. His mastery of choral writing is also evident in his operas, and at the other extreme in amusing and sometimes improper catches. Purcell established choral music of the highest quality in a new, and more free, environment.

7

The "Hallelujah" and other Choruses

FOR more than 200 years general appreciation of choral music has stemmed from one chorus, composed by George Frideric Handel (1685–1759) in the late summer of 1741. This is the "Hallelujah" chorus in the oratorio *Messiah*, which was first performed in Dublin, on April 13, 1742. A year later *Messiah* was heard for the first time in London. Present at the first London performance was the King, George II, and since he was moved to stand up when the chorus burst in with the opening bars of "Hallelujah", the entire audience, out of politeness, had to do so too. The practice of standing for the "Hallelujah" chorus was maintained until recent years, and even now it is by no means unknown.

The thought of a king standing up to show his respect for a musician (or for God, or for both) naturally made a deep impression, especially in England where the idea of showing respect to musicians was unfamiliar. It added a romantic touch to a story that was already more than half way to popularization. It was believed by many that one day, while Handel was busy writing the "Hallelujah" chorus, his servant entered his room, whereupon the composer said that he was seeing a vision of the heavens opened, the angels singing, God on his Throne and so on. This anecdote is added to many more that accumulated around the person of George Frideric Handel to impress his image indelibly on the British people.

When Handel composed *Messiah* he had in mind a small group of singers—of boys and men from a Cathedral choir. In fact, when he went to Dublin he had two choirs at his disposal, those of St. Patrick's and Christ Church Cathedrals (although a number of singers belonged to both choirs); even so there were no more than forty singers. In the last years of Handel's life, his oratorios, and particularly *Messiah*, were being sung at festivals in many towns in England. These performances were organized around professional cathedral choirs. But in the year of the composer's death, there were performances in the Universities of Oxford and Cambridge, and in the important midland city of Coventry. In the autumn of that same year, an enthusiastic clergyman in Leicestershire organized a Handel festival—of which *Messiah* was the main part—in his village church of Church Langton.

A few years later William Mason was able to note how "the rage of oratorios had spread from the Capital to every Market Town in the Kingdom". In 1784 the Centenary of Handel's birth (according to the old calendar, displaced in England in 1752, Handel was born in 1684) occasioned a Commemoration in Westminster Abbey. This was a mammoth affair, with 500 performers taking part. It was very successful and similar events were organized in 1785, 1786, 1787 and 1791. On each occasion large forces were employed, and the idea grew that the more performers there were the better the music sounded. Handel became the composer of the masses, sung by many, listened to by many, approved by all. Originally this unprecedented popularity was established in Britain; but before the end of the eighteenth century it had spread to North America and northern Germany. As a result music was never quite the same again; for it had been finally wrested from the grasp of the aristocracy.

Handel was a great opportunist. In general, he appreciated what was wanted and supplied the demand. He was born in Germany (the German form of his name is given on page 80) and brought up within two musical traditions: the one of Lutheran church music, with its connections with civic music; the other of Court music—especially that of Weissenfels near his birthplace of Halle. Lutheran music meant primarily church cantatas in various forms, and Handel was taught by one of the masters of this branch of music—Friedrich Wilhelm Zachau (1663–1712). Court music, although with secular cantatas similar to those of the church but in honour of the Duke rather than of God, primarily meant instrumental music. This latter was much influenced by Italian sonata and concerto style.

Memories of Lutheran music not infrequently stirred in Handel in later life, sometimes consciously and sometimes unconsciously. A chorale melody was introduced into the *Funeral Anthem* (really a cantata, with several movements) composed after the death of Queen Caroline in 1737. A psalm setting by an unfamiliar German composer (see Ex. 10 on p. 80) is recollected in "Lift up your heads", in *Messiah*. The way in which Handel set the words "And peace on earth" to a monotone was anticipated by another German composer; while the main theme of the "Hallelujah" chorus is strikingly similar to that of a chorale. The text of the air "I know that my Redeemer liveth" had been set by many German composers since the sixteenth century, and was, indeed, one of the most frequently used texts in Lutheran church music. There is a beautiful solo cantata by Georg Philipp Telemann (1681–1767), which was once incorrectly ascribed to J. S. Bach entitled "I know that my Redeemer liveth".

Handel left Germany, however, and went to Italy in 1706. He remained there for more than three years. During this period he not only learned all about Italian music at first hand, but made a reputation for himself as a fine composer well able to compete with the best Italian composers in their own style and on their own ground. He composed operas, cantatas, and church music. In 1707 he composed settings of Latin Psalms

in Rome, and in the next year an oratorio. *The Resurrection,*
in the then fashionable Italian oratorio style.

In Italy, Handel learned the effectiveness of florid, *coloratura*
singing, whether by solo voice or by the choral unit as it was
then constituted. He perceived the value of direct and clear

EX. 18

expression, and of the possibilities of interlinking voices and instruments in the manner, more or less, of concerto. The examples of music for voices by Carissimi, Caldara, and Leo on pages 105, 107 and 109, are not by Handel; but all of them have qualities that could be recognized as Handelian.

The smooth counterpoint of the Carissimi example on p. 105, traditional in the way the voices are spaced and treated in respect of progression, but forward looking in its theatrical feeling, anticipates many choral movements by Handel that are in fugal style. One fugue of Handel which has the classical qualities that came down from the sixteenth–seventeenth centuries is the "Amen" of *Messiah*. Emotionally charged chromatic notes such as we have found in Leo (see p. 109) are also to be found. There is a fine and telling passage in *Israel in Egypt* that indicates the "thick darkness" that was sent "over all the land" of Egypt. In a mournful chorus in *Judas Maccabaeus* chromatic notes are also used to great effect (Ex. 18).

Choruses in a style as fluent and brilliant as that of Caldara abound, though Handel's range of brilliance is wider, and he was less inclined to be repetitive. The following example may be compared with that from Caldara on p. 107 (Ex. 19).

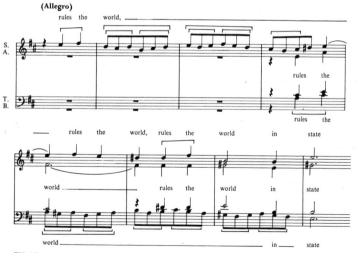

EX. 19

What is particularly notable in Handel's choral music is its dramatic quality. A song should transfer into musical terms ideas that are present in the words which are the basis of the song. Handel was the first composer to unify words and large-scale choral music in a similar manner, and so effectively that the message immediately gets over to a general audience. Of course, the great composers of choral music who preceded Handel as well as those who were his contemporaries affected their audiences. But they were addressing themselves to more or less restricted audiences. Handel, in his prime, wrote music for a much wider public, and it was on the approval and affection of that public that he prospered.

The German-born Handel went to Italy, as has been said, where he sharpened his tools and extended his range of techniques. In 1710 he arrived in England, and in a short time decided to make his permanent home there. Seventeen years later he became a naturalized British citizen.

The greatness of a composer naturally depends on his own gifts, determination and perception; but it also depends on being in the right place at the right time. England was a country with a strong choral tradition. Other countries had their own choral traditions but that of England was much more intimately associated with the language of the people than was the case in many other lands. There was no longer any competition from Latin, while an attempt to foist Italian on to the British people (truthfully, only those who were in London) was rapidly frustrated.

Some part of the frustration was Handel's. He came to London, at the suggestion of certain members of the aristocracy, with the intention of supplying the town with Italian operas—then the rage all over Europe. At first he enjoyed considerable success, but interest quickly lessened. A persistent individual and a composer who took great pleasure in composing dramatic music, Handel went on to write some forty operas. But while he was doing so he caught hold of other interests, brought them together, and established the tradition of the English oratorio.

Let us see what these other interests were. In the seventeenth century, musical attention in the English church was concentrated on the anthem, on special occasions enlarged to the scale of a miniature cantata, with instrumental interludes and accompaniments, passages for solo voices and fairly extensive sections for chorus.

Handel picked up the English tradition from Purcell, and other composers, and was enabled to extend it when called upon to write his *Utrecht Te Deum* and a *Birthday Ode* for Queen Anne in 1713.

In these works Handel gave enough to his chorus singers to make them feel grateful to him. These singers formed a fairly close corporation. The top voices were supplied by choirboys—who did what they were told. The men belonged to the Chapel Royal and to St. Paul's Cathedral, some being members of both choirs. On big occasions the choristers of both foundations combined forces. They also worked together in a society—the Academy of Vocal Music—that had been set up in 1710. A sociable man, Handel got to know these singers (as also the instrumental musicians of London) well, and being on excellent terms with them was encouraged to write the kind of music that best suited them. In 1718 he composed twelve anthems for the Duke of Chandos. These anthems, thereafter known by the Duke's name and his only effective memorial, were sung by some members of the Chapel Royal Choir hired out to the Duke, as also were a little pastoral work, *Acis and Galatea*, and a large-scale sacred work later known as *Esther*. To all intents *Esther*, a musical setting of a dramatic story from the Bible, was an oratorio. But it was not yet classified as such.

Esther was first performed in 1720, then for a time it was forgotten. Handel went on composing all sorts of other music. In 1732, however, the Master of the Chapel Royal Choir, thinking that *Esther* was far too good a work to be lost, revived it—as a birthday present for its composer. At that time, feeling against

[122]

Italian singers, Italian opera and the Italian language, was running high in London. Friends of Handel suggested that he should try to evolve something similar to Italian opera, but with English words. What he did do was to bring together the opera and the anthem tradition, and it was from this union that the distinctive type of oratorio, that was to become so popular in England, was born. The great advantage of this form was that it respected the English love of the Bible, gave moral satisfaction by reason of its basis of religion, engaged the interest of the best available solo and chorus singers and, at the same time, satisfied the general need for "a good story".

With the exception of *Messiah* and *Theodora* (which was, however, a Christian story) all the sacred oratorios of Handel were taken from Old Testament sources and were settings of extremely dramatic subjects. In all Handel composed some seventeen sacred oratorios, of which the best-known are *Israel in Egypt* (1739), *Judas Maccabaeus* (1747), *Messiah, Samson* (1743), *Saul* (1739), *Solomon* (1749), and *Theodora* (1750); and about ten works of similar structure to oratorio, but secular in character. Of these the most familiar are *Acis and Galatea* (1719), *Alexander's Feast* (1736), *L'Allegro* (1740), and *Semele* (1744). The words of these were taken respectively from John Gay, John Dryden, John Milton, and William Congreve. Congreve wrote *Semele* as an "English opera" in 1704, but it was not until Handel became interested in the subject that it had music worthy of the theme.

In all of the works the choral element is of the greatest importance. In *Israel in Egypt*, much of which is composed in eight parts for two groups of S.A.T.B. singers, there is little other than chorus music. In every case, Handel uses the choruses descriptively or dramatically, so that many subjects are brought within the scope of choral observation. The range is limitless— from the high-voiced welcome of David by the young Israelite women in *Saul* to the dark mourning music of *Judas Maccabaeus*; from the merry village strains in *L'Allegro*, by way of the "nightingale" chorus in *Solomon*, to the vision of the "celestial concerts" in the finale of *Samson*. *Israel in Egypt* is a stupendous "wide-screen showing" of almost every conceivable choral effect. For the ordinary man the choruses of *Messiah* are a comprehensive catalogue not only of Christian but also humanitarian philosophy. This is music with which many generations of music lovers have identified themselves. It is also music on which choral societies were based, and the means whereby music became effectively democratized. And at its heart lies the "Hallelujah" chorus in *Messiah*. This is not, in fact, the only "Hallelujah" chorus in Handel's works, there being others in the First and Fourth Coronation Anthems (1727), *Deborah* (1733), and *Athalia* (1733); but it is enough to be going on with.

In so far as it was possible in the first half of the eighteenth century, Handel was a composer of world stature. In the Germany that he had left they still remembered him, and held him in high regard. Occasionally he went back to Germany, sometimes to engage singers for the opera, sometimes for family reasons. On two occasions, a German musician who had never been outside his own country made unsuccessful attempts to meet him, once in 1719 and once ten years later. This was Johann Sebastian Bach (1685–1750). Bach had a great regard for his contemporary and made copies of one of Handel's Italian cantatas and of his *Passion* music of 1716—which was written for performance in Hamburg. Bach considered Handel a great man. Handel, however, had no idea of the greatness of Bach as a composer. Nor had many other people.

Bach belonged to a good, solid, Thuringian tradition of professional music. Like his forefathers, his eldest brother Johann Christoph (1671–1721), and his cousins, he was church organist, Court musician, and Cantor. At every stage of his career he was intimately concerned with choral music. Within the limits of German music (and it must be remembered that Bach never left Germany) he brought to a noble conclusion the traditions belonging to the Lutheran Reformation, the bicentenary of which was celebrated during his lifetime.

As a schoolboy in Eisenach (he went to the school at which Martin Luther had been a pupil), Bach sang in the choir of St. George's Church of which Johann Christoph Bach (1642–1703), a fine composer of organ music and motets, was organist. When his father—Johann Ambrosius (1645–95), town musician in Eisenach—died, Johann Sebastian was taken into the household of his brother Johann Christoph, at Ohrdruf. Here again, as a pupil at the Grammar School, Bach sang in the church choir. A fine singer, he became an object of interest to talent scouts from northern Germany, and was taken into the famous school—with a fine choir—in Lüneburg. Here he was able to hear music performed by the Court musicians of Celle (who also played in Lüneburg) and to visit Hamburg—the most celebrated musical city of the north.

In 1703 Bach returned to his native Thuringia, where, in quick succession, he was a court musician (and valet!) at Weimar, and organist in Arnstadt and Mühlhausen. At this stage he was well informed in the standard music of the Lutheran repertoire—from the sixteenth-century masters to newer composers like Thomas Selle (1599–1663), of Hamburg, Georg Kühnhausen (d. 1714), of Celle, both of whom had composed popular settings of the *Passion*, and Johann Kuhnau (1660–1722) and Johann Schelle (1648–1710), famous Cantors of St. Thomas's School, Leipzig. Schelle composed a "Christmas Oratorio", which had some influence on the later work of that order by Bach himself. But there was one musician, of whom he had heard much while in northern Germany, whom he particularly wished to meet and hear. This was Dietrich Buxtehude (1637–1707).

Buxtehude had for many years been organist of St. Mary's Church, in Lübeck. A feature of the musical life of that city were the five big concerts which were given each year in the church, by choir and orchestra, on the five Sundays before

Christmas. These concerts, described as *Abendmusik* (evening music), had been instituted at the suggestion of the merchants of Lübeck in the middle of the seventeenth century.

The programmes included organ music (Buxtehude was a famous organist and composer of organ music), motets (many written by Buxtehude) of splendid proportions and for a wide variety of voices and instruments, and other religious music, but also some secular music. In 1700, for instance, a seasonal, non-religious, piece, *Winterlied* (*Song of Winter*) was performed. So keen was the young Bach to experience this music at first hand that he begged leave of absence from his organist's post at Arnstadt, and walked (or, with the help of friendly wagoners, hitch-hiked) to Lübeck. Once there—in an atmosphere free from the perpetual interference of Dukes that characterized life in Thuringia—he was not anxious to leave. When he came back to Arnstadt he found himself in disgrace with his employers for having overstayed his leave. Very soon afterwards, Bach moved to Mühlhausen, and shortly after that accepted a more attractive post as musician (not valet, this time) to the Duke of Weimar. He remained in Weimar for nine years, until 1717.

During this first period of his professional life, Bach established himself as the finest organ player in Germany, and his reputation in this respect obscured his genius as a composer. Actually, except in the towns where he worked, there was not any reason for him to be widely hailed as a great composer, as his works, almost entirely, existed only in manuscript. He had written motets and church cantatas before he went to Weimar. When he was there he was required to provide a new work each month. From this period, there remain about thirty church cantatas as well as some secular cantatas.

From Weimar Bach moved to Cöthen, as Director of Music to the local Duke, and he stayed there until 1723. At Cöthen the official religion was that of the Reformed, i.e. Calvinist, church, and even though the Duke was unusually tolerant of other creeds, Bach had relatively little opportunity to write church music. It was during this period that he composed the greater part of his orchestral, chamber and keyboard masterpieces. In 1723, however, he applied for and was appointed to the cantorship of St. Thomas's School, Leipzig, a post which involved the direction of most of the musical activities of the city, including the University.

In anticipation of his appointment Bach composed the *St. John Passion*, which was performed in St. Thomas's Church in 1723. Within a year he wrote the *Magnificat* (to the Latin text, since Latin was still used for parts of the Lutheran liturgy), the funeral motet *Jesu meine Freude* (*Jesu, my Joy*), and a number of cantatas. During the next three years or so, he composed at least three complete cycles of church cantatas, and a number of secular cantatas, as well as other music. In 1728, the *St. Matthew Passion* was composed, and performed the following year. Five years later the major part of the *Mass in B Minor* was delivered to the new Elector of Saxony, August III, from whom Bach sought the title (which eventually he obtained) of Royal Music Director. In this capacity he wrote music that sounds positively Handelian (showing common ground on which both composers stood). The opening of a ceremonial chorus for the Elector is given in the following example. What Bach did not say was that he had written this years before, in honour of a professor at Leipzig University (Ex. 20).

EX. 20

In 1734, the *Christmas Oratorio*—which is a set of six cantatas to be performed on different days during the period of

Christmas—was composed. Between 1729 and 1740, Bach directed the important concerts of the musical society known as the *Collegium Musicum* and was rather less active as a composer of church music. The bulk of the choral works with which we are now familiar today, therefore, belong to the first years of his career in Leipzig, although he added more cantatas to the list in his last years and also revised some earlier works.

Of the works mentioned in the last paragraph, some are now regarded not only as masterpieces of choral music but as among the greatest works in the whole realm of music. Two hundred years ago, however, they were all but forgotten; and even during the composer's lifetime they received no general, wholehearted acclamation.

This was due partly to the fact of Bach's supreme gifts as executant—which were appreciated. More particularly, however, changes of attitude and taste were responsible.

The musical tradition of Lutheran Germany had depended on the co-operation of educators, and on the provision of adequate time for basic music instruction in the timetables of the Grammar Schools. Bach himself had been brought up under such conditions and saw no reason why they should be changed. But, in the interests of progress, they were changed. When he was at Leipzig, Bach fought a running battle with the authorities of St. Thomas's School to retain his authority and also to maintain satisfactory working conditions. The next illustration shows the present-day choristers of this school, rehearsing in the Church of St. Thomas.

It is to be remembered that his greatest works were written for the boys (and young men students) of St. Thomas's School, from whom also the soloists were drawn. When we consider that these works now tax the powers of the best professional singers it is a testimony to the boys and to their sometimes justifiably irritable teacher that they were able to give any kind of passable performance. The orchestral parts, let it be said, were played by a handful of professionals augmented by

amateur musicians and students. In Hamburg, where Telemann was Music Director, the resources of the Opera House were available. In London Handel had the pick of the considerable professional talent available. Bach, in comparison, was much less fortunate. There was no resident opera in Leipzig, and church music was not held in the same esteem as formerly.

This brings us to another important point. Church music was less important in that theology had declined in significance, at least so far as the intellectuals were concerned. Religion was institutionalized but in place of the old dogmatic assertions a broader rationalism, and humanism, were in vogue. Bach lived through the period of the "Enlightenment", in which the leaders of German thought and social practice aspired to the philosophic excellence of the French and the aesthetic brilliance of the Italians.

This not only affected Bach's way of life—especially in Leipzig, the "German Parnassus" or the "Little Paris" as it was called towards the end of Bach's life—but also the character of his music. Italian influences had made themselves felt long before Bach's day, and especially in the works of Heinrich Schütz. But the practices of the Venetian school of the Gabrielis slipped naturally into the established textures of Thuringian and Saxon music, adding spaciousness and enhancing instrumental tone values. The influences of fully developed Italian opera, however, made for a more radical change. Emphasis on recitative and aria (the three-section aria which can be shown as *a b a*), and on the solo voice, meant less emphasis on the choral element.

At the end of the seventeenth century, the conventions of opera invaded church music. Erdmann Neumeister designed libretti for church cantatas which stressed recitative and aria; although to be fair, the central role of the chorale was maintained. The intention was to make religious instruction both modern and attractive. Other librettists followed Neumeister's example. Salomo Franck, who provided cantata texts for Bach in Weimar; Christian Friedrich Henrici (known as "Picander"); and Mariane von Ziegler, who wrote libretti for him in Leipzig. As librettists these once famous writers were not nearly as efficient at the job as those who drafted the oratorio books for Handel in London.

Notwithstanding the character of the texts with which he was provided (often he altered them to bring them into line with his orthodox religious beliefs), Bach cancelled their frequent sentimentality and obscurity by going behind the words to uncover the basic truths of religious experience. As we now see it, these were also the basic truths of human experience. Thus such works as the *St. Matthew Passion* and the *Mass in B Minor* fulfil the intention of the founders of the Christian Church by being of an universal significance. They are, then, complementary to the great works of Handel.

Handel was always aware of his public. He was, therefore, careful to write in such a way that performances were practicable. He was a superb master of vocal and instrumental techniques and never wrote music that did not sound right, that is, right for the medium. Moreover, he wrote with the theatre in mind. His oratorios were performed not in church but in the opera house and the atmosphere was transferred to the quality of the music.

With Bach it was otherwise. As a composer of vocal music he had in mind the choristers of the many churches he had known since childhood. He also kept in mind the precepts that he had learned from the lips of village and small-town pastors when young. There were mysteries in life; but beyond these mysteries lay the truth. To solve the mysteries meant wrestling with them; it often induced pain and suffering; but at the end of the period of trial there was a divine assurance. It was the stress that he placed on the effort needed to understand the problems of life (and religion) that gave to Bach's choral writing its particular character.

The source of this aspect of Bach's art lay in the Thuringian motet and chorale that had been familiar to him since his school days, and which had extended into fine and striking works in the hands of earlier members of his family. The motet style of writing is seen at its best in the six motets composed in Leipzig, four for eight, one for five, and one for four voices. Chorales were woven into these, most strikingly in the case of *Jesu, meine Freude*, which is, in effect, a series of variations on a chorale. In many of the cantatas, as in the *St. Matthew Passion*, and the *Christmas Oratorio*, whole movements are designed in the manner of organ chorale preludes, with the harmony, and, more particularly, the counterpoint designed to interpret and even to symbolize the words. Of such cantatas one of the best known is that based on the stirring Reformation hymn, *Ein feste Burg*. But Bach was as alive to the new as to the old, and he made use of the structure of the Italian *concerto grosso* (he was a keen student of the music of Antonio Vivaldi) in choral music. Splendid examples of this are the opening choruses of the *Magnificat* and the *Christmas Oratorio*.

Singers find Bach inexhaustible. He has become as much a twentieth-century as an eighteenth-century composer. This is for two reasons. Firstly, he set out life through music in strenuous terms. Secondly, he energetically set about trying to solve

EX. 21

its perplexities. Among the great composers Bach is one of the most rhythmic. There is a kind of cosmic rhythm underlying his musical utterances, such as the slow pulsation that underlies the Incarnation in the *Mass in B Minor*: (Ex. 21).

In the opening of a cantata for Michaelmas (No. 19) about the war in heaven described in the Revelation of St. John, another aspect is shown. This same story had, years before, been described by Johann Christoph Bach in a motet from which Johann Sebastian took some hints (Ex. 22).

The influence of Handel carried straight on. That of Bach went underground, to re-emerge later.

EX. 22

8

Changes of Direction

Most of the choral music performed (or recorded) at the present time is old rather than new. This, of course, applies to instrumental music. But there is a difference. Many of the choral works that are in the current repertoire belong to the period that ended with, or about, the death of Handel. The most popular instrumental works, even taking into account an increased interest in music of the seventeenth and of the first half of the eighteenth centuries (the Baroque period) are those which were composed after the death of Handel and up to the end of the nineteenth century. For many centuries, the most important part of Western musical tradition had been contained in music for voices. Gradually instrumental music had caught up with vocal, so that by the time of the great masters described in the previous chapter there was, in many forms, a nice balance between the two. In the second half of the eighteenth century, however, instrumental music drew ahead in popularity, and the dominant musical form was that of the symphony. In 1782, Johann Samuel Petri, a German musician of conservative inclination, complained that the near-eclipse of church music by symphony, concerto and opera, was a "great catastrophe". However, as is said, you cannot stop progress.

Choral music depends on group activity, on the submission of individual ideas to those of a corporate body. Those who sang in the choirs of cathedrals, monasteries, and royal chapels, in the so-called "golden age" of choral music are mostly unknown to posterity. Those who are known owe the fact to their talent as composers. In the existing records of foundations, it is possible to discover the names of choir singers, because their appointments and wages were noted, but by themselves the names give little indication of the lives they led. With the solo singers who began to come into the forefront of musical affairs after the great changes that took place in music in the early seventeenth century, there is a good deal easily to be discovered about them.

The truth is that, after the establishment of what was optimistically called the "new music", the value of the individual as an individual became a central point of philosophy, with considerable consequences not only for the arts but also for society. In brief, this is what the Renaissance and the movement known as the "Enlightenment" were about. In the eighteenth century this brought into question the nature of God, even the existence of God, and, if there was such a Being, the relationship of man with Him. At the heart of this lay the matter of freedom—the freedom of the individual, the freedom of the group within society, the freedom and independence of the nation. These matters are still central to philosophy, religion and politics.

The pursuit of freedom led towards a new appreciation of nature, which the eighteenth-century poets often viewed as a vital spiritual force in itself. Feelings about nature, and feelings (or emotions) in a general way, were viewed with increased respect. Music was expected to do two things: to "imitate" nature; and to convey emotions. These principles were shared by many theorists. Apart from opera, the kind of music thought most effective in achieving these aims was that for orchestra, and the symphony evolved in accordance with this philosophy. The way in which melody was treated, often seemingly as an end in itself, was symbolic of the significance of the individual.

Inevitably the traditional forms of choral music looked out of place in these new conditions. Except for the music of

Handel, to which further reference will be made, the bulk of the music so far described in this book was pushed back over the side lines. Palestrina was performed by the Sistine Choir; sixteenth-century masses and motets were occasionally to be heard in the larger Roman Catholic churches of Europe; motets and cantatas of earlier periods were still sung in some German churches; and anthems of William Byrd and Orlando Gibbons were sung in English cathedrals. But these vestiges of survival, except in the case of the Sistine Chapel where a strict, unchanged doctrine concerning "sacred music" prevailed, were due to the occasional resilience of a conservative spirit among a minority or to considerations of economy. It was cheaper to go on using old books than to buy new ones.

As a matter of form, choral foundations were kept up in churches, monasteries, and cathedrals, and for that matter, also in nunneries, but during the eighteenth century standards fell. The great musicians of the post-Baroque period were no longer those who held church appointments.

We may then appreciate that during this period the great division of music into secular and sacred took place. The last great composer to see no such division was J. S. Bach, who, devoutly Christian, and in many ways—outside music—conservative, saw the world and humanity as wholly part of the mind and will of God. So much did Bach feel this unity that he used the same music for secular and for sacred cantatas, without any complaint on the part of the religious. A generation later, the Masses of Mozart scandalized some and delighted others because they were said to be "operatic" in style.

Within the field of religious music there were, however, fresh developments resulting from the general shake-up of philosophical and social attitudes. In England, the crusade of John Wesley (1703–91) aided by his brother Charles (1707–88), split the established Church of England. Those who formed themselves into the Methodist Church were, for the most part, the underprivileged to whom Wesley offered a "hope of salvation" that did not seem likely to be available from any other quarter. Like all great religious movements, Methodism built up its own heritage of song, and during the second half of the eighteenth century many new hymns—usually distinguished by their emotional qualities—were composed. Charles Wesley, who was very musical, wrote as many as 6,000 hymns, a large number of which have been set to music by a variety of composers. The Wesleys were inspired to this work by the example of the Moravian missionaries whom they met while working in the mission field in Georgia, U.S.A. The earliest hymns of the Methodists were translated from German originals, and they show strong traces of the influence of the German Pietist and Brotherhood movements.

In due course, Methodist Churches were built, and choirs were formed to lead the singing of the hymns. These choirs, especially in the North and Midlands of England, and in Wales, were almost entirely working-class in membership, and were to exercise a powerful influence on the development of choral music. To meet the new demand a large number of hymnbooks were published in England during the eighteenth century.

In the meantime similar democratic forces were at work in America. As has been seen on p. 113 the foundations of congregational singing were laid in America by the immigrant Puritans of the seventeenth century. Towards the end of that century psalm and hymn singing was in a bad condition. In 1721, John Tufts led the way in reform by the issue of his *Introduction to the Singing of Psalm-Tunes*, in which he used a simplified manner of printing music, which he thought would be easier for those who had had no previous training to grasp. He went right back to the methods of Guido d'Arezzo, using sol-fa syllables and placing them on the lines and in the spaces of the stave (see illustration on p. 114.). In doing this he was in advance of John Curwen (1816–80), who did not popularize his system of sol-fa notation in Britain until the middle of the nineteenth century.

In 1761 James Lyon (1735–94), a Presbyterian minister born in Newark, New Jersey, published a "Choice Collection of Psalm-tunes, Anthems, and Hymns" entitled *Urania*, in which were tunes familiar in the English psalm books, but also some that were American in origin. What was important about Lyon's work was that it also contained "directions for singing". Though these would appear now as somewhat elementary, they were very useful when they first appeared.

During the last years of the eighteenth century, the most original voice in American music was that of William Billings (1746–1800), a tanner in Boston, who was a self-educated composer. His principal interest was sacred music, and he attempted to combine the popular psalm style with the more formal methods of German music and composed what he called "fuguing pieces". He was indifferent to "rules", and was only concerned with expressing his thoughts. His anthems and hymns are more distinguished by power than by charm.

In 1770, Billings published what became known as a "musical declaration of independence". This was a volume entitled *The New England Psalm Singer*, with original tunes to replace those that had come down from the Bay Psalm Book. Eight years later, he issued *The Singing Master's Assistant*, with melodies which Billings said had "more than twenty times the power of the old slow tunes". A vigorous fighter in the revolutionary cause, but by music rather than the gun, Billings was a stirring parodist. His hymn tune "Chester" inspired those fighting for independence when it swept across the eastern seaboard. The words, of which the first verse follows, were written after the manner of the metrical psalm.

> Let tyrants shake their iron rod,
> And Slav'ry clank her galling chains,
> We fear them not, we trust in God,
> New England: God forever reigns.

Billings, the forerunner of such composers as Charles Ives in his handling of musical material, crusaded for music for the common people of a new nation. This was the voice of America, in 1794, from Billings's *The Continental Harmony* (Ex. 23).

EX. 23

Music inspired by the example of Billings was composed by Abraham Wood (1752–1804), of Northboro, Mass., also a prominent figure in the struggle for independence, who is remembered for his *Columbian Harmony* (1793) and his last work, *Elegy on the Death of General George Washington* (1800).

The ideal of liberty, which culminated in the French Revolution, was alive in many hearts during the eighteenth century. Not least of all far across Europe in Hungary, where the Magyar people, sick of centuries of oppression both by the Turks and Austrians, made a number of attempts to gain their freedom. Music, which had always been a means of expressing national pride among the Hungarians, played its part. Again it was music associated with a Protestant religion. In 1743, a professor in the Calvinist College in the ancient city of Debrecen reorganized the choral section of the Musical Society of the College, with the intention that its members should sing, not in Latin, nor in German, (the language of the alien Austrian rulers) but in their own tongue. In order to facilitate this he published a choral book entitled an *Abridged Method of Harmonic Singing*, which was part of the inspiration of the great revival of Hungarian music that took place during the late nineteenth and twentieth centuries.

In one way or another, then, the idea that the principles of liberty and freedom could effectively be expressed and spread through mass singing took on a new lease of life.

At the same time, there was a considerable development in social singing. This was particularly the case in Britain, where singing clubs grew up in large numbers. From the Academy of Vocal Music (see p. 122) a Madrigal Society grew in 1741. Its founder was John Immyns, a lawyer, who was less concerned with reviving an old form of music than with showing that madrigals were one of the best forms of recreational singing. Immyns himself copied out parts. Among the members of the Society according to the historian, Sir John Hawkins, who was a member—were working-class people—"mechanics . . . weavers . . . [and] others of various trades and occupations".

Although we speak of a "revival" of madrigal singing it should be remembered that the art was not really entirely forgotten. Pieces such as Morley's "Now is the month of Maying" and Wilbye's "Flora gave me fairest flowers" continued to be sung—but often those who sang them in the eighteenth century were indifferent both to the fact of their being madrigals, or to the existence of a huge body of other similar part songs. The difficulty, of course, was that the old part books were not in general circulation; and if they had been, singers of the eighteenth century would have had difficulty in copying with the by now unfamiliar clefs and melodies set out without bar lines.

John Immyns made copies (not always very accurate) that had bar lines. A little later, John Stafford Smith (1750–1836), a friend of Hawkins, made a more detailed study of the works of the madrigalists, and he acquired sets of part books. After his death these were sold by auction. In 1844, Thomas Oliphant (1799–1873) also a keen madrigalian, purchased a whole lot at a ridiculously low price for the British Museum, which has an unrivalled collection of sixteenth- and seventeenth-century part books.

Twenty years after Immyns started the Madrigal Society, a Noblemen's Catch Club was founded in London and, in imitation, similar societies sprang up all over Britain. Many composers were kept busy writing glees, catches, canons, even madrigals and so on, for the enthusiastic members of such clubs. They were encouraged by the award of prizes, and also by the fact that publishers were anxious to obtain as much of this kind of sociable music as they could lay their hands on. The composers were by no means limited by subjects that were thought proper for musical treatment. So we find many slices of real life exhibited: (Ex. 24).

This is a catch in three parts, by Samuel Webbe (1740–1816),

1st Voice

I've seen, I've seen I've seen a box-ing match to - day, I've

seen, I've seen a box-ing match, I've seen, I've seen a box - ing match a

box - ing match to - day, — and faith a good one too

EX. 24

with one voice entering after another. The counterpoint gives
a very good idea of the in-fighting that went on during this
contest. The story ends:

> A countryman was in the fray,
> Who struck each blow so true.
> So black and hairy was his breast,
> His back so broad and brawny
> That in the first heat with ease
> He beat the other to a tawny.

Other choral music was required for a society known as that
of the Freemasons which had come into being during the
eighteenth century, and which included a certain amount of
ritualistic music during its ceremonies.

At the present time, many towns in Britain and the U.S.A.
have "Lodges" of the Freemasons, and music still plays a part
in the ceremonies.

All this is a far cry from the main channel of "classical
music". But, eventually, these various forces had a profound
effect on the development of such music; and especially on the
development of choral music.

The conventional appreciation of musical history is made
easier by assuming that composers worked according to some
prearranged scheme. So there is a tendency to imagine that

[142]

when Bach and Handel disappeared from the Baroque scene, the curtain came down, and that when it went up again it did so on a new act representing the "Classical period" in which the heroes were Josef Haydn (1732–1809) and Wolfgang Amadeus Mozart (1756–91). This too-facile simplification leaves out of account certain important particulars.

For better or for worse Bach and Handel were working in environments in which the taste of the middle classes had an effect on the kind of music provided. Haydn and Mozart on the other hand, were in the first place obliged to consider the opinions of the aristocracy. As subjects of the Austrian Empire they were conditioned by the principles of absolutism in government. They did, or were expected to do, what they were told. Haydn was a liveried servant of the Court of the Princes of Esterház for the greater part of his career. He was fortunate in being able to accept the situation and also in enjoying, thanks to the good will of the Excellencies who employed him, tolerably pleasant conditions. Mozart, son of a musician to the Archbishop of Salzburg, was for a time a member of the same staff as his father. When, however, he found that the conditions were degrading and intolerable, he resigned. By so doing he consigned himself to a life of poverty. In order to live at all, he was unwillingly compelled to try to keep on terms with the Austrian Court, and the aristocracy in general, in Vienna. He gave lessons, took part in private concerts, and wrote works for which he was sometimes paid and sometimes not. In those days there were no royalty payments on the sale of music, and no performing rights fees. The composer who had no fixed post was dependent on the good will of rich patrons.

Austria was a stronghold of Catholicism, and during the seventeenth and eighteenth centuries many splendid Baroque churches were built. Richly adorned, with paintings, sculptures and silver and gold ornaments, these churches had a theatrical quality which affected the character of church music. Also, opera being the chief entertainment of the aristocracy, whose

[143]

sense of piety was unimpressive, it was natural that the principles of operatic music should be freely admitted into church music. The more like opera the music of the Mass sounded, the better pleased was the audience. As has been seen, the influence of Italian opera was considerable even in northern Europe; in Austria, next door to Italy, it was irresistible.

Haydn himself was a chorister in the Cathedral of St. Stephen in Vienna. The choir of that church was also the choir of the Royal Chapel, having been founded by Maximilian I, in 1498. The same choir still exists, and the performances now given in St. Stephen's by this choir and the Vienna Philharmonic Orchestra attract many visitors. At St. Stephen's, Haydn was brought up on the ancient style of Palestrina and Lassus (whose music was reserved for the penitential season of the church year). He also learned the scientific, contrapuntal music of Johann Joseph Fux (1660–1741)—now better known as a theorist than as a composer, and the eloquent works of Caldara and Reutter (see p. 107). The latter was his teacher. Haydn's younger brother Michael (1737–1806) was also a pupil of Reutter, and since he became a church musician (organist to the Archbishop of Salzburg) the Austrian style of church music may be appreciated also in his works. Michael held more closely to the stricter polyphonic tradition than Joseph, so that his works seem in comparison more old-fashioned. A fine composer, of equable temper, he only lacked the outstanding genius of his brother, for which reason he has been rather unjustly neglected.

Josef Haydn wrote his first Mass at the age of eighteen in 1750. Thereafter, for a time, he devoted himself to instrumental music, particularly to string quartet and symphony. In 1761 he was appointed to the Court of Esterház. His duties there included the writing of Masses, and other church music, for the Prince's Chapel. There were two kinds of settings of the Mass, the one for ordinary Sundays, the other for Festivals. The former was described as a *Missa brevis* (Short Mass, but not to be confused with the Lutheran *Missa brevis* which consisted only of the first two sections, "Kyrie" and "Gloria"); the latter as a Festal Mass, which was longer and usually scored for larger orchestra.

Both Haydn and Mozart composed Masses of both types. They set the text, as a rule, for a quartet of solo singers and for choir, the two groups being contrasted after the manner of a *concerto grosso*. A feature of the vocal writing of both composers is the brilliance of the solo items, which were designed for the best available opera singers. Both composers were also aware of the flexibility of the symphony and the larger movements are often set in symphonic manner.

In a Catholic country, opportunities to compose church music come frequently. Haydn composed for the Chapel of his Prince, for the Royal Chapel in Vienna, as well as for private individuals, religious societies and the Musical Society in Vienna. Mozart composed Masses for the Archbishop of Salzburg (who ordered that none should take longer than half an hour in performance), and for various chapels, shrines, and, again, private persons.

The "sacred" music of both composers, therefore, covers a wide range. Not only because of the variety of circumstances in which works were written, but also because of the rapidly increasing importance of the orchestra. The earliest Masses of Haydn used instrumental forces that were familiar to Bach and Handel; his later Masses, on the other hand, employed the orchestra as it was known to Beethoven. Haydn composed fourteen Masses as well as much other church music. One of the most charming of these is the "St. Nicholas" Mass of 1772— a Christmas Mass in honour both of St. Nicholas and Prince Nicholas of Esterház (see illustration p. 146). The finest of the later works of this kind are the "Creation" and "Windband" Masses of 1801 and 1802 respectively. The "Creation" Mass is so-called because it quotes a theme from the duet of Adam and Eve in the oratorio *The Creation* (see p. 152). In the

"Wind-band" Mass we see how completely the form of the instrumental sonata had been completely absorbed by the composer into choral music, and how, by implication, the music of the world had conquered that of the church. In other words, these later Masses of Haydn had little or no connection with any requirements of the liturgy. The point was not lost on later Popes who, according to tradition, at various times tried to put the rein on composers of church music.

Mozart's Masses, like those of Haydn, were composed for

many different occasions, and differ widely in scale. Of the larger Masses the most brilliant is the so-called "Coronation" Mass of 1779. This was composed for an anniversary celebration in the church at Maria Plain, a mile or two outside the city of Salzburg. The particular anniversary was of the placing in the church of a picture of Madonna and Child—miraculously saved from destruction by fire at Regen, in Bavaria. In his Mass, Mozart marvellously contained the spirit of the inborn devotion of the Austrian people to the legends of the faith, the pomp of a great occasion and the glitter and extravagant beauty of a Baroque church. Far away, at another extreme, is the *Requiem Mass* which he composed during the last few months of his life.

Mozart was a theatrical composer. He was also a dramatic composer. He was a master of comedy, but also of tragedy. The *Requiem Mass*, written in response to a commission from a nobleman who wished to pass himself off as a composer by buying a score from Mozart, was left unfinished, and was put into final shape according to Mozart's sketches and annotations by Franz Süssmayr (1766–1803). Süssmayr was a pupil of Mozart.

As in Haydn's latest works, one is struck by the variety of instrumental effects in Mozart's *Requiem*—particularly by the dark colouring of trombones and of the *corni di bassetti* (tenor clarinets). One is also reminded of the dignity of the older contrapuntal methods of composing church music, particularly as shown in the massive opening movement.

A composer at any time uses the style to which he and those around him are accustomed. But he reserves the right to vary this style, to modify it by reference to other styles, to revert to traditions that have temporarily become unfashionable. To the best of his ability, a composer keeps many lines of communication open. Austria was not Germany, and the traditions of the Austrians and the north Germans were different. In the eighteenth century, however, clever musical craftsmanship was esteemed regardless of its origin. Scientific music, as it was called, appealed to teachers all over Europe. The chief "scientific" form was that of fugue. The acknowledged master of fugue was J. S. Bach.

In Austria, since little of Bach's music was published, his reputation mostly depended on hearsay. But a nobleman, Baron Gottfried van Swieten (1734–1803), Austrian Minister at Berlin from 1771 to 1778, had ample opportunity of getting to know the works of the German composers at first hand. He returned to Vienna, and immediately spread around his enthusiasm for Bach and Handel. In 1782, Mozart arranged five fugues by Bach for string quartet and the influence of that master became apparent in his own compositions. In 1788 Mozart visited Leipzig and heard the great motet for double choir "Sing ye to the Lord" in St. Thomas's Church. He asked to see the scores of other works by Bach. "Here," he said, "for once, is something from which we may learn."

Although conditions of life were different in Vienna from those in Berlin, or Hamburg, or London, or Boston, or New York, at the end of the eighteenth century, music spilled over the frontiers so that what happened in one city affected the musical health of another. Thus, in Vienna, musical life was enriched by traditions that had established themselves in London, while the foundations of musical culture in America were the works of Handel and Haydn. This was due to the way in which musical affairs were organized.

9

The Oratorio Cult

UNTIL about 1770 (the year in which Beethoven was born), musical performances by modern standards were on a small scale. After that date, however, the dimensions both of performance and composition were greatly increased. The long-held idea that music was an aristocratic privilege, which had been under strain for a long time, finally arrived at the point of collapse.

By 1770, the Subscription Concerts that were general all over Europe and in America—even though often patronized by the aristocracy—were open to a wide middle-class public. This was a period in which, except for opera, the accent was on instrumental music. It was the period in which the form of the symphony was established and the basic shape of the "symphony orchestra" settled. The orchestra of 1770 was not only larger than that of a few years earlier, but more varied in its sonorities; the woodwind, brass, and percussion instruments were assuming more prominence and gaining more independence. The aim of the musician, according to theories that were widely held, was to "imitate nature", and to express and to stimulate the emotions. When these theories were placed in the context of the changes in society and in musical organization stated above it is clear that a change in the nature of music is inevitable.

In broad terms, this change is usually described as the

transition from Classical to Romantic values. So far as choral music is concerned, this transition, with its many implications, can be understood in human rather than in technical terms. In 1770, the most important choral works, designed for the most part for small groups of professional singers, were presented to the public. Thirty years later, choral music of the stature of Haydn's *The Creation* and *The Seasons* existed so that the public, or a representative body of the public, could take part in its performance. In 1770, choirs were twenty-, thirty- or forty-strong. By 1800, the membership of choral societies was in the hundreds, and women were at last admitted as members.

Originally this expansion of choral activity was based on the oratorios of Handel. These established themselves in Britain not only as musical works but also as the means whereby charities could benefit. During Handel's lifetime, his works had been used for charitable ends. The proceeds of the first performance of *Messiah* were devoted to helping the poor, the sick, and the prisoners of the city of Dublin. In London, annual performances of the work were, at Handel's wish, given in aid of the Foundling Hospital. During the latter part of the eighteenth century, partly through the energies of the Methodists, the conscience of the British middle class was awakened to social inequalities and injustices, and charitable organizations were set up in large numbers. Many of them were concerned with the building of hospitals. For more than a century, there was hardly a hospital built in Britain that had not derived some of its funds from performances of Handel's oratorios.

The starting point of the large-scale Handelian performance was the Commemoration of 1784. At this performance, singers from the provinces were drafted into the chorus. When these singers returned home, they set about organizing regional festivals on an ambitious scale. During Handel's lifetime festivals of his oratorios (in whole or in part) had taken place with some regularity in towns such as Salisbury and Bath. The feature of the Handel cult of the later eighteenth and early

[150]

nineteenth century was its extension to the great manufacturing and commercial cities of the north and the midlands. Leeds, Sheffield, Newcastle, and Birmingham, became focal points for oratorio performances. The participating choristers were drawn from church and chapel choirs, from the middle and the working classes. The impact made by such performances was considerable.

It should be remembered that in Britain the only regular professional orchestral organizations were in London. The provinces, unlike the provinces of Germany, were more or less devoid of orchestral performances of high quality, while productions of opera were almost nonexistent. Choral music, therefore, was the most important part of general musical experience. When Handel's oratorios were given, it was customary to bring down from London the soloists, the leaders of the orchestra, and often the conductor. Local patriotism thus was concentrated on the quality of the chorus, and a good deal of rivalry grew up between various towns.

In the early part of the nineteenth century, all this activity which had been focused on occasional oratorio performances, was regularized by the institution of choral societies. By the middle of the nineteenth century, there was not a town that did not take pride in its choral society.

The Commemoration of 1784, from which all this directly flowed, which helped more than anything else to stimulate choral music at that time had other consequences. Its success led to later performances on a similar scale in Westminster Abbey. In 1791 Josef Haydn, visiting England for the first time, was present at the Handel performances in the Abbey. The music of Handel was not unknown to him, since Baron van Swieten had arranged performances of his oratorios, but on a small scale and in his own house. Haydn had never heard such overwhelming choral music in his life. He was completely bowled over by the force of Handel's choral genius. "Handel," he is reported to have said, "is the master of us all." Three years later he heard part of another Handel Festival in London, and went home to Vienna inspired with the general idea of Handelian oratorio.

In 1775, Haydn had composed an oratorio in the Italian style—*Il ritorno di Tobia* (*The return of Tobias*)—for the Musical Society of Vienna. It was not greatly successful, for the oratorios of Italian composers, and of the Italo-German master Johann Adolph Hasse (1699–1783) were more in line with the taste of the Viennese. After his English experiences, however, Haydn determined to attempt a large work in the Handel manner, with much emphasis placed on the chorus.

The text of *The Creation*, based on Milton's *Paradise Lost*, was prepared for him by Baron van Swieten, and the oratorio performed for the first time in the Palace of Prince Schwarzenberg on April 30, 1798. The audience, unlike those in London, was a fashionable one. But everybody who could was determined to be present to hear what Haydn regarded as his greatest work. To cope with the numbers expected, the authorities of Vienna cleared away the traders' stalls in the adjoining New Market so as to prevent traffic congestion! *The Creation* was a great success, and in response to the general enthusiasm two more performances were arranged.

The choral writing in *The Creation* owes much to Handel. It is spacious and dramatic. There are recitatives and arias, and duets and trios for the solo singers. These sections often run on into choruses, as in the case of "The Lord is great", where thrilling effects are achieved by the soloists singing more elaborate passages over the chorus parts. In "The Heavens are telling" choral and solo passages alternate. The choral writing is made dramatic by exciting changes in the dynamics and also by the introduction of striking and unexpected changes of tonality. The tonal changes encountered, for instance, in the duet and chorus "By thee with bliss" are similar to those that Haydn employed in his symphonies and string quartets.

The Creation also owes to the symphony its extensive

orchestra which was, indeed, larger than used for symphonic music—of double woodwind, double bassoon, two horns, two trumpets, three trombones, drums, and strings. The orchestration plays its own part in enhancing the work and the wide range of effects help to broaden the choral expression. It is not possible to sing in a choir backed by such a force without reacting to the instrumental stimulus.

The theme of the creation of the world is, by any standards, a great theme, one which we can only begin to think of with difficulty. It is a theme of universal concern and its elemental quality makes it suitable for discussion in Haydn's generous terms. It is music for a large choir.

Three years after he had given *The Creation* to the world, Haydn, at van Swieten's suggestion and again to a libretto by van Swieten, presented another oratorio (a secular one) at the Schwarzenberg Palace. This was *The Seasons*—a popular subject for musical treatment since Vivaldi had written his cycle of descriptive *concerti grossi* on the same subject. Purcell had dealt with Spring, Summer, Autumn, and Winter in *The Fairy Queen*. Bach's librettist, Christian Friedrich Henrici, had written a charming cantata (probably the music, that is lost, was by Bach) on the same subject that was performed in Leipzig in 1727. But Haydn's *The Seasons* was the first large-scale treatment of what again is a universal theme. In this work, Haydn pictures the peasant life that he knew so well in the Burgenland province of Austria where he had been born and had lived for most of his life. He had been on the friendliest terms with the peasants who worked near Rohrau and Eisenstadt, and in the country running down to the Neusiedler Lake. In this work, Haydn made use of the contrast between women's voices and men's voices, as in the opening chorus and the later "Hark the mountains resound" and "Joyful the liquor flows".

With this work Haydn finally pushed the oratorio form from a religious to a worldly setting. In doing so, although he was a devout Christian, he reflected the tendency of the Romantic age. The romantic urge of music lovers in England had been stimulated not only by musical works but also by the circumstances surrounding works. The picture of Handel, aged and almost blind, attending a performance of *Messiah* a few days before his death did much to confirm the sentimental hold of that oratorio on the affections of the English.

So far as *The Creation* was concerned, people in Vienna also remembered how Haydn attended a performance in the University not long before his death. He, too, was old and infirm, and had to be carried into the concert hall. When the chorus burst out with the words "Let there be light", there was spontaneous and prolonged applause. Haydn lifted his hand and said, "It is not from me, it all comes from above." Such anecdotes come more easily, perhaps, in respect of choral works; and certainly they have their effect on the imagination of singers who sing not because they have to, but because they want to. A composition of the kind of *The Creation* takes music into a new, and fresh, environment. Haydn's oratorios quickly took their place by the side of Handel's in the British choral repertoire.

But the Handel-Haydn merger (as it became) also had a profound effect on the musical life of the people of the United States.

On December 25, 1815, after strenuous months of campaigning and rehearsing, the Handel and Haydn Society of Boston gave its first public concert. The programme consisted of large excerpts from *The Creation* and *Messiah*, with miscellaneous items from other oratorios of Handel as well as a glee (another name for a part song) by the currently popular English glee composer, Samuel Webbe, who had come into prominence in 1794 when he had won a prize in London at the Catch Club. The establishment of the Boston Handel and Haydn Society was a triumph for its founder, Dr. George K. Jackson (1745–1822), an Englishman and a former choirboy of the Chapel Royal in London, who emigrated to America in 1796.

Jackson had sung in the tenor section of the choir of the 1784 Handel Commemoration in London. A number of orchestral players who had taken part in that festival also emigrated to America and helped to lay the foundations of instrumental music across the Atlantic. Jackson worked both in New York and Boston, as organist and teacher, and his ambition always was to set up in his new country the kind of choral institutions that he had known at home. When he arrived in America choral singing was in a rudimentary state, and there were no groups able successfully to undertake the choruses of Handel and Haydn.

The difficulty, as has already been suggested, was lack of training. The church choirs were mostly indifferent, hardly competent even to do justice to the music of the psalm books or the choruses of William Billings. During the later part of the eighteenth century attempts were made in various towns to improve the general situation. In Bethlehem, Pennsylvania, a Moravian colony was established, which carried on the German tradition of music as best it could. In the middle of the century, a *Collegium Musicum* was founded there, which existed until a Bethlehem Philharmonic Society was formed in 1820. One Moravian, John Antes (b. 1740), went to Europe where he became acquainted with Haydn personally. It is believed that at the beginning of the nineteenth century both *The Creation* and *The Seasons* were performed in Bethlehem.

In 1784, Andrew Adgate (d. 1793) founded an *Institution for the Encouragement of Church Music* in Philadelphia and in 1786 conducted *A Grand Concert of Sacred Music* for the benefit of the Pennsylvania Hospital, the Philadelphia Dispensary, and the poor of the town. A body of 230 singers was assembled. The works performed were mostly long-forgotten pieces by local composers but Handel was represented by the "Hallelujah" chorus. The foundations laid by Adgate were built on by Benjamin Carr (1768–1831) to whom was owed the establishment of the Musical Fund Society (1821), under the auspices of which the first important choral performances were given in Philadelphia. But it was in Boston that the most consistent choral development took place.

Jackson was fortunate in arriving there when a sound musical culture had been developed in the life of the city by the organist William Selby (1738–98), who had directed occasional performances of Handelian choruses by the choir of King's Chapel, and by Gottlieb Graupner (1767–1836), an instrumental musician who had come to Boston from Hanover.

To form a good choir, however, was uphill work. When Jackson announced his intention, there was a response from forty-four singers—most of whom belonged to church choirs and had taken part in previous concerts at which Jackson had performed isolated oratorio choruses. By the time the first concert was given, the membership had grown to ninety—of which only five were women! The concert, however, was very successful and the Handel and Haydn Society went from strength to strength. The choir grew to 150 (twenty women). Solo singers from Europe were introduced to the Boston public and oratorio concerts became a regular part of the concert life of the city.

Music in America in those days relied greatly on the stimulus brought to it by immigrant musicians. At first, these were mostly of British origin; but the number of German musicians quickly increased, so that, during the nineteenth century, their influence on the American scene was very great. In the meantime, however, German music had also undergone revolutionary changes, which substantially affected choral music.

The solid core of German music remained in the Lutheran Church, and the old traditions were zealously and carefully protected by Cantors and organists in countless small towns and villages. They were inspired by memories of a great past held in the manuscript collections that were still often used, and by the fine music performed under the direction of great musicians in the principal churches of the important cities. In Hamburg, all the music of the city was in the hands of Telemann until his death in 1767, when it passed into the hands of Carl Philipp Emanuel Bach (1714–88), whose reputation in Germany was hardly less than that of his father. Wilhelm Friedemann Bach (1710–84), the eldest and, it was said, the most gifted of the sons of Johann Sebastian, was a church musician for a time in Dresden and Halle. A third brother, Johann Christoph Friedrich (1732–95), director of music at the little North German Court of Bückeburg also maintained the family tradition of church music. To the sons of Bach may be added their cousins—in Ohrdruf, in Meiningen, in Eisenach, and in many other towns and villages—who, revered because of their name, strove to justify themselves as members of what by now was the most famous musical family in Europe.

All these men composed settings of psalms, motets, oratorios, Passions, and so on. To a varying degree they held to the established contrapuntal methods that they had been taught, but by placing more emphasis on elegant lines of melody— more economical in decoration than was the case in the Baroque period—and emotionally effective harmony and instrumentation, they pushed church music in the direction of secular music. Especially in the larger towns, the performance of church music was much more of a concert performance than a part of the church liturgy. At the same time it would be difficult to find choral music of this kind that was not marked with a sense of the serious purpose of music. However much German composers might be influenced by French or Italian manners, they were rarely able to disguise their nationality.

The zeal that was bestowed on choral music is illustrated by the instructions given by Johann Samuel Petri in a long section of his *Anleitung zur praktischen Musik* (*Introduction to practical music*), published in Leipzig in 1782. Petri makes it clear that he is writing not with the professional singers of the Courts in mind (who would laugh at his simple advice, he says), but with those of the "town choirs". By town choirs he meant church choirs, since they were always available for civic music.

[157]

He also gives some idea of the average size of such choirs when writing of bodies of "two or three dozen singers".

It is doubtful whether a better guide to the techniques of choral singing has ever been written. Petri, himself a teacher of singing, had at his disposal the fund of common sense that is the choral director's chief ally. For instance, he advocated putting the trebles and altos (boys) at the front of the choir because they were smaller than the men. The tenors, he suggested, should be placed near to the violas and the second violins, so that they could be helped by the fact that in fugal movements these instruments would be playing their parts. He proposed that since the tenor voice was the strongest in ensemble, fewer tenor than other singers were necessary. In the event of the tenors being insufficient, however, he would transfer some of the deeper-voiced altos and some of the higher basses (baritones) to the tenor section. In general—and here he was speaking of the tendencies in the music of the time at which he was writing—the outstanding parts should be the treble and the bass. But whenever a chorale appeared in the texture of a work this should be given proper emphasis.

Petri assumed that the chorus singers were good sight readers, accurate in intonation, and well informed about the theory of music. He said therefore that singers should notice which notes in a melody should stand out (in his view, the 1st, 3rd, 5th, and 7th degrees of the scale). He advised that before performing any work each singer should look through the whole work to appreciate its general character and to know in advance where difficulties were likely to occur. He was a firm believer in good phrasing, and sustained singing. Recognizing that an efficient breath control was the basis of good performance, he told his readers to watch out for the best places to take breath, warning that it was sometimes necessary slightly to shorten the end note of a phrase in order effectively to tackle the next.

The director of the choir, seated at the harpsichord, must himself be a singer. Strategically placed, he would pass on his

[158]

tempi to the principal first violinist, on his right, and to the solo 'cellist on his left, who would in turn keep the orchestral forces in order. When solo singers were involved, the director, playing the main part of the accompaniment on the harpsichord, supervised their rhythm by discreet movements of the left hand. It was all very much a team effort.

Petri summed up the solid, thorough methods of generations of choirmasters, whose habits were scrupulous even when their talents were slender. The extent to which every detail was covered is illustrated by the fact that Petri marked a table on his layout of choir and orchestra, on which extra strings for string players unlucky enough to break any, and spare copies of music for the singers and instrumentalists, could be conveniently kept ready for use. (See diagram below.)

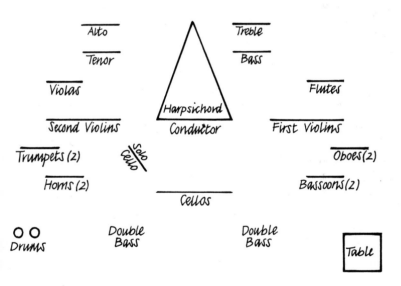

All of this, perhaps, is what is meant when one speaks of a "musical tradition". This is the foundation on which generations of composers built.

When Telemann went to Hamburg he had the firm intention to make music available to as many people as possible in as many ways as possible. He wrote and published numerous works for amateurs to play and to sing. He also wrote instructional works. But what proved to be of greatest importance in the long run was that he organized regular series of concerts for the general public, as he had done previously in Frankfurt. At the *Collegium Musicum* (as it was still called) Telemann performed works of every kind; instrumental concerts, and suites, songs, church and secular cantatas, scenes from operas, works composed for occasions of local importance, and oratorios.

Hamburg had a firm connection with England, due to mutual trading interests as well as cultural links which were also strong. In the eighteenth century a musical connection was maintained by the enthusiasm of the British Ambassadors (John Wych and, after his death, his son Cyril) for the Hamburg Opera on the one hand, and the fact that Johann Mattheson, a friend of Handel and Telemann, and also Secretary to the British Mission was married to an Englishwoman. From time to time, musicians from England visited Hamburg. In 1771, Michael Arne (1740–86), son of Thomas Arne (1710–78) came with a singer, Miss Anne Venables (whom he later married) to give some concerts. These concerts were given with the good will of the Hamburg musicians, of whom Carl Philipp Emanuel Bach was now the head.

On September 23, 1771, Arne directed a performance of Handel's *Alexander's Feast*. On April 15, 1772, he performed *Messiah*. This work, then unknown in Germany, was a revelation, and at the end of December, 1775, Carl Philipp Emanuel Bach gave a performance of the work. The German text had been prepared by the poet Friedrich Klopstock (later translations were by Johann Herder, in 1781, and Johann Adam Hiller in 1786). Among those present at this performance was the great composer Christoph Willibald Gluck (1714–98), who was completely bowled over by the power of the music.

The report of the Hamburg performance was spread abroad; in 1777 *Messiah* was performed in Mannheim, in 1780 in Schwerin and Weimar, in 1786 in the Cathedral in Berlin and in the University church in Leipzig. The Berlin and Leipzig performances were conducted by Johann Adam Hiller (1728–1804), who had prepared the German text. Inspired by reports of the London performance of 1784, Hiller used large forces both in Berlin and Leipzig, there being not less than 200 performers on either occasion. Thereafter, *Messiah* became as much a part of the German as of the English musical tradition. Handel, who had lived the last fifty years of his life away from Germany and had died a British subject, became a national hero. He has remained a national hero in both countries.

Hiller is one of the most important figures in German music. A pupil of the Kreuzschule in Dresden he went to Leipzig in 1758. He re-established musical life there after the Seven Years War which ended in 1763, and founded the famous Gewandhaus Concerts. In 1771, he established a singing school and took a great interest in choral music generally. In addition to the works of Handel, he revived older music and brought J. S. Bach back into the repertoire. For his oratorio performances he relied mostly on the choristers of St. Thomas's Church (of which he became Cantor in 1789), but both by his own compositions, his teaching, and his general enthusiasm, he made amateur musicians aware of the riches that were available to them in the choral repertoire.

Meanwhile, amateur singing was going strong in Berlin where Carl Friedrich Fasch (1736–1800) formed a choir, of women and men, from among his pupils. Fasch belonged to a typical German musical family. His father, once a pupil at St. Thomas's School, Leipzig, had been active as concert promoter in Leipzig and as director of the music in the town of Zerbst. Carl Friedrich was fortunate in being appointed to the music staff of Frederick the Great when a young man. For more than forty years he was at the heart of things in Berlin.

The King believed that music should continue to play a prominent part in the life of the community. He also believed that it had a part to play in building up a sense of national pride. To this end, he encouraged music on every level. During the last quarter of the eighteenth century nationalism was a strong force in Germany, and particularly Berlin. Bach and Handel began to be described not only as great musicians, but also as among men whose words and deeds were to be the foundation of a unified nation. In 1793, a writer in a magazine —Gentz's *Deutsche Monatschrift*—described J. S. Bach as the Orpheus of the German people. Eight years later in a musical journal, the *Allgemeine Musikalische Zeitung*, there were four references to Bach. In one he was compared with Homer, in another with Michelangelo, in a third with Albrecht Dürer, and in the fourth with Isaac Newton. In 1802, Johann Nikolaus Forkel (1749–1818) who had been a choirboy in the same church in Lüneburg as Bach and had directed music in the University of Göttingen for many years, published the first biography of Bach. What better way of presenting Bach to the widest possible public, by means of the new choral societies.

The Singakademie (as it was called) in Berlin was formed out of Fasch's choir of pupils in 1792 and given royal patronage. In 1794, motets by Bach were performed. In the next year Handel's *Judas Maccabaeus* was added to the list of his works that were in the German repertoire. In 1800 when Carl Friedrich Zelter (1758–1832) succeeded Fasch as director of the choir, Mozart's *Requiem* was given a public performance.

Now, as so often in the past, the life of Germany was upset by war. The Napoleonic Wars swept across Europe and the threat to Germany was only removed by the defeat of the French at the Battle of Leipzig in 1813. As a result, there was a great upsurge of patriotism and of patriotic feeling. All of this was reflected in attitudes to choral music and in the new music that was composed for singers.

10

Choral Music as a Social Force

THE nineteenth century was an age of mass movements. This was partly due to the consequences of the Napoleonic Wars which heightened a sense of nationalism throughout Europe, partly to the increasing tempo of industrialization, and partly to fresh social impulses that sprang from a combination of both.

In every European country, societies—some political, some cultural—were formed, to nurture national ideals. The expansion of industry, leading to a conflict of interests between employers and employees, eventually gave rise to the setting up of organizations for the protection of workers. As a result of these developments, education assumed a greater importance than ever before. The historic and cultural traditions of nations were popularized through education; political, religious and social stability were, it was hoped, to be secured through educational systems; at least a minimum of education was necessary for the great majority who would furnish the workers needed to carry through the massive programmes of industrialization that were to characterize the nineteenth century.

In many countries music was an important part of the national heritage. Musical activity in general was often seen to lead to both religious and social stability. On the other hand, according to long tradition, music was also an aid to those whose attitudes were unorthodox. The nineteenth century was also the age of the great choir. For the first time, the choir of several hundred voices became the norm of choral expression. Having arrived at a choral body of such dimension almost by accident, as described in the previous chapter, and having discovered the thrilling effects created by vast numbers of singers, a virtue was made of sheer size. There was a tendency to consider that a choir (and, for that matter, an orchestra) was good because it was big.

It should, however, be remembered that the choral societies of the age gave opportunity to hundreds of thousands of modest music lovers to become acquainted with many of the masterpieces of music at first hand. Further, there was an incentive to composers to write new works. Some of the finest works in the choral repertoire belong to the nineteenth century.

The foundation of choral music in the nineteenth century was provided by Handel and Bach. Already secure in the affections of the British people, Handel's oratorios were the basis of the Festivals that took place in the great industrial towns of the north and the Midlands, and of the Eisteddfods (singing competitions) that, in new form, inspired the singers of Wales. In order to accommodate Handel to the local forces that had become the rule rather than the exception, his scores were edited so that the fuller resources of the then modern orchestra might be used to support the choirs the like of which Handel had never known. Re-orchestrating Handel was, however, not particularly a practice of the British. The first to put "additional accompaniments" to *Messiah*, for instance, was Mozart (for performance at Baron van Swieten's), and German musicians were not backward in "improving" not only on Handel but also on Mozart, and, before long, they went in for bringing Bach's orchestration up to date. In the twentieth century, the general tendency is discreetly to avoid the excesses of nineteenth-century editors. While this, no doubt, is proper it should not be forgotten that through their enthusiasm and energy the nineteenth-century musicians did great service in the cause of popular musical culture.

[164]

The peak of the popularization of Handel in England was represented by the mammoth festivals that began (after a trial run in 1857) in 1859, the centenary of Handel's death, in the Crystal Palace, London. These Festivals went on until 1926 and the number of performers engaged in each was about 3,000–4,000. The kind of tone produced by a choir of several hundred, or several thousand, is undeniably thrilling. It is, however, often a glutinous kind of tone that lacks the clarity that is necessary for the linear music of the Baroque era. With music of the nineteenth and twentieth centuries, it is another matter. Composers adjusted their ideas, as will be seen, to new conditions. But Handel and Bach, etc., were hardly able to do this. If they had known what was to come they would, no doubt, have written rather differently from the way they did.

Once started, the cult of Handel in Germany grew stronger and stronger and, in 1856, it was proposed to establish a Handel Society with the principal aim of issuing the works of Handel in scholarly editions. (A short-lived Handel Society with the same aim existed in England from 1843–8, and a number of scores were issued.) The inspiration for this great work came from Friedrich Chrysander (1826–1901), whose researches are the foundation of all modern Handel scholarship.

In America, Handel and Haydn ran in joint harness, under the powerful influence of the Boston Society. From time to time, this Society was kept in touch with the European tradition of choral singing through immigrant musicians. One of these was Aaron Upjohn Hayter (1799–1873), who was organist at Grace Church, New York, and at Trinity Church, Boston, where he became organist of the Handel and Haydn Society in 1837. Before coming to America Hayter had been organist of Hereford Cathedral, and conductor of the Three Choirs Festival. Founded in the early eighteenth century, this was the oldest of musical festivals, and remained faithful to the Handel tradition. The three choirs originally were those of the cathedrals of Hereford, Worcester and Gloucester. In the nineteenth century the choristers were augmented by the choral societies of the three cities.

There is nothing like an anniversary for stimulating action. In 1817, the German Lutherans celebrated the third centenary of the Reformation. Falling soon after the end of the Napoleonic Wars, as a result of which nationalism grew more intense, this anniversary naturally focused on choral music. In Hamburg, in addition to performances of liturgical music in the churches, a performance of Handel's setting of *Psalm 100* and parts of *Judas Maccabaeus* was given by an amateur choir. The promoter of this performance was Louise Reichardt, (1780–1826), daughter of Johann Friedrich Reichardt (1752–1814), a musician and a scholar, who was one of the first to revive choral music of the sixteenth and seventeenth centuries, in Germany. He helped in the affairs of the Singakademie in Berlin, of which his daughter, a singer and composer, was a member. As a result of the Hamburg performance, a Singakademie was established in the city. Other towns in northern Germany followed suit.

After the death of J. S. Bach, his reputation largely rested in his instrumental music (which was all that was published during his lifetime), and his choral works were largely ignored. It is to the credit of the English Bach enthusiast Samuel Wesley (1766–1837) that the first nineteenth-century concert performance of one of the motets, *Jesu meine Freude*, took place in London, under his direction, on June 3, 1809. But much credit for the revival of interest in the great choral works goes to Felix Mendelssohn (1809–47), whose performance of the *St. Matthew Passion* in Berlin, on March 11, 1829, was a turning point both in the history of choral music and in the posthumous reputation of Bach.

Mendelssohn possessed a copy of the score of the *St. Matthew Passion* (of which the original was in the possession of the Berlin Singakademie), and his interest was stimulated in Bach both by Zelter, one of his teachers, and by Goethe on whom he had made a good impression in Weimar. It is to be noted that

[166]

Zelter, a "scientific" composer after the Berlin manner, was accustomed to composing in the "old" style of Bach and he wrote masterly preludes on chorale themes.

With Zelter's permission, which was readily forthcoming, Mendelssohn gave his performance of the *St. Matthew Passion* at the Singakademie. He made cuts, and he replaced the obsolete instruments of the oboe family—the oboe *d'amore* and the oboe *da caccia*—with clarinets. The interpretation in general was in a romantic style. The impact made by it was, however, considerable. Soon afterwards, performances took place in Breslau and Königsberg, and, in 1830, the *Passion* was published. Within five years the work was heard for the first time in Frankfurt, Stettin, Kassel and Dresden. At Kassel, the Elector of Hesse was unwilling to allow his orchestra to be used for a work of which he disapproved; so Ludwig Spohr (1784–1859), Music Director in Kassel and a famous conductor and composer, had to make do with pianoforte accompaniment. In 1833 in Dresden things went to the other extreme. The orchestra numbered 112 players—with forty-six violins, ten double basses, eight oboes, and eight clarinets—and the choir was 230 strong.

The *St. John Passion* was revived in Berlin in 1833. Parts of the Mass in B Minor, which had already been heard in Frankfurt, were performed also at the Singakademie in 1835. Johann Mosewius (1788–1858), founder of the Breslau Singakademie, devoted himself to performing Bach's church music and through his performances, drew attention to the beauty and variety of the church cantatas. He published pamphlets on Bach's church music in general and on the *St. Matthew Passion* in particular in 1852. In Leipzig, a statue of Bach was erected in 1843, largely through Mendelssohn's exertions, at the side of St. Thomas's church. Meanwhile the publication of Bach's choral works had been progressing through the influence of Johann Gottfried Schicht (1753–1823), Cantor of St. Thomas's from 1910–23, and the interest of the Leipzig publishing house of Breitkopf and Härtel. In 1850, a Bach Society, similar in aims to the

Handel Society already mentioned, was formed. Among the sponsors of this Society was Robert Schumann, whose respect for Bach is shown in the fine set of *Fugues on the name B.A.C.H.* for organ and in the wonderful final chorus of his almost forgotten choral work based on Goethe's *Faust*.

With characteristic thoroughness the music of Bach, once re-established, was protected by many Bach societies set up in various towns in Germany. Such a society was founded in Hamburg in 1855, and others followed in Leipzig, Heidelberg, Göttingen, Wiesbaden, Cöthen and so on.

Mendelssohn, a frequent visitor, was almost as well known in Britain as in Germany and his playing of Bach's organ works nourished the enthusiasm of such Bach lovers as Samuel Wesley. In 1837, Mendelssohn persuaded the authorities in Birmingham to include part of the *St. Matthew Passion* in the Birmingham Festival. Other works began to make their appearance in London programmes through Mendelssohn's sponsorship, and in 1849 a Bach Society was formed. The founder was William Sterndale Bennett (1816–75), who had been friendly with Mendelssohn and Schumann while he was a student in Leipzig.

In 1870 Joseph Barnby (1838–96), conductor of a choir promoted by the publishing house of Novello, performed the *Christmas Oratorio* at a London oratorio concert. In the next year he gave the *St. Matthew Passion* both in St. Anne's Church, Soho, and in Westminster Abbey. Later, in 1871, Barnby succeeded Charles Gounod (1818–93) as conductor of the Royal Albert Hall Choral Society (with which his original choir was amalgamated) and the *Christmas Oratorio* and the *St. Matthew Passion* were at once included in the repertoire.

In 1875 a group of London singers met to study the Mass in B Minor, which, conducted by Otto Goldschmidt (1829–1907), was performed in St. James's Hall, on April 26, 1876. Goldschmidt, born in Hamburg, was a pupil of Mendelssohn in Leipzig, before settling in England. So successful was this performance that the choir decided to stay together. That is

how the Bach Choir in London came into being. Since its foundation many celebrated English musicians have been its conductors, among them the composers Charles Villiers Stanford (1825–1924) and Ralph Vaughan Williams (1872–1958).

Although emphasis has so far been laid on Bach and Handel, and, therefore, the Protestant Anglo-German tradition, it must be remembered that there was another tradition, that of Catholic church music. Music for the Mass, in particular, was strongly maintained. Through the publication of the Masses of Haydn, Mozart and Beethoven (and, frequently, the alteration of words to suit non-Catholic consciences), this tradition met the other in the concert hall. The major work from within the Catholic tradition was Beethoven's *Missa Solemnis*.

Beethoven composed a *Mass in C*, in 1807, at the request of Prince Nicholas Esterházy (Haydn's employer). It was received with disapproval. Beethoven, lavishing his imagination on the text, had set the work in what was then a modern style.

If a composer wishes to please the majority of those who listen to sacred music, he is best advised not to introduce a too-modern style. Regardless of convention, however, Beethoven wrote as he felt he should, and while the *Mass in C* (for soloists, choir, and orchestra) will not seem strange to us, it did seem strange to the Esterházys. As far as they were concerned it was devoid of recognizable melodies, and the shifts of harmony were more or less meaningless. Eleven years later Beethoven began to compose another Mass, in honour of the elevation of his friend the Archduke Rudolph to an archbishop's throne.

But the Archbishop had long been enthroned before Beethoven completed the work. This is a measure of the difference between a composer of the nineteenth century and those of preceding ages. Previously, any composer would have been thoroughly ashamed of himself if he had not completed a work on time. He would also have been concerned if what he had written had not proved immediately practicable.

Using the full resources of virtuoso soloists, chorus singers, and symphony orchestra, Beethoven, however, posed many problems because of the new relationship established in this Mass between voices and instruments. The instruments are as important as the voices, not merely illustrating the words but, as it were, exposing the atmosphere lying behind the text. This is particularly noticeable in the section "Et incarnatus est", where the strings are reduced in number and the flute given a high and decorative part; in the prelude which introduces the "Benedictus", and in the trumpet and horn parts that dramatically interrupt the "Dona nobis pacem". The way in which the vocal parts merge into the orchestral and are continued by the instruments show that this Mass is a truly symphonic work. In the relationship between voices and instruments it may be seen to bring back certain principles from the "sacred symphony" of the seventeenth century.

The Mass in D is said to have been performed privately in St. Petersburg at the request of Prince Galitzin. On May 7, 1824, part of the work was given, together with the Ninth ("Choral") Symphony (in which voices are introduced into the last movement to sing Schiller's *Ode to Joy*), in the theatre in Vienna. The first complete performance took place, at Warnsdorf, in Bohemia, on June 29, 1830. Two years later the first English performance took place at the home of Thomas Alsager in London. The soprano part, about which the German singer Henriette Sontag had complained to Beethoven on account of its difficulty, was sung by the fourteen-year-old Clara Novello (daughter of the founder of the publishing house), who was to become one of the greatest oratorio singers of the nineteenth century.

Although Beethoven's Mass, by reason of its dimensions, is unsuitable for performance within the liturgy and is, therefore, generally to be heard under concert conditions, it belongs to the Catholic tradition because of its general atmosphere. In the narrow sense it may not be "religious", but in the broad sense it is devotional.

Other works of the first part of the nineteenth century which continue the tradition of the Baroque Mass are the settings of Franz Schubert (1797–1828), Gioacchino Rossini (1792–1868), and Charles Gounod. Somewhat later, the Austrian tradition was enriched by the fine works of Anton Bruckner (1824–96).

The expansion of choral music that took place during the nineteenth century would have been less marked had it not been for the energy of publishers and of educators. So far as the publishers are concerned pride of place should go to the London firm of Novello, which was expressly founded with the intention of making the great masterpieces of choral music available to the greatest number of people at the lowest cost. Of musical educators the most conspicuous in this field were Guillaume Wilhem (1781–1842), Joseph Mainzer (1801–51), and John Curwen (1816–80).

Wilhem, a Frenchman, had a genius both for teaching singing and for organization. As musical superintendent of the municipal schools of Paris, he revolutionized the teaching of music and, through his classes, he inspired great enthusiasm for choral music which led to the institution of choral societies throughout France. Mainzer, a German of radical opinions, was obliged to leave Germany after 1830 on account of his revolutionary tendencies. He, too, went to Paris, where he started singing classes among the working people. In 1841 he arrived in England and found fertile ground for his work. He settled in Manchester, and preached the gospel of choral music among the working classes in the north. John Curwen's great contribution to choral music was the standardization and popularization of the sol-fa system, which proved a godsend to all those who, although inadequately equipped by formal musical education, wished to take part in singing the standard oratorios. Choirs in working-class communities became very proficient by means of sol-fa. This was particularly marked in Wales, where rivalry between choirs became fierce. Cups—such as that shown in the next illustration—were competed for with great zest, and are to this day.

Mainzer and Curwen exercised a considerable influence on the musical education of children, both in day schools and Sunday schools. Sunday schools provided the singers for many Victorian church and chapel choirs, as well as choral societies.

THE LONDON SUNDAY SCHOOL
CHOIR
AT THE ROYAL ALBERT
HALL

An illustration of a Sunday School Choir festival concert is shown on the previous page.

At this time choral music often depended on the efforts of non-professional musicians. This was particularly the case in America. Lowell Mason, a New Englander, was a bank official with a great love for music, especially hymns. Self-taught, he learned to compose hymn tunes and many of them enjoyed considerable popularity. For a time Mason led the church choirs of Boston, where he also served as President of the Handel and Haydn Society for five years. He was, however, deeply concerned that music should play a proper part in public education. Inspired by the methods of the Swiss educator Heinrich Pestalozzi (1748–1827), and the Swiss musician and publisher Hans Georg Nägeli (1773–1836), Mason applied these methods in Boston. Basically his teaching rested on thorough teaching of the elements of theory and of sight reading and the provision of suitable material. Like all the other pioneers of general musical education, Mason edited and issued suitably graded collections of music. His views were not only respected in his own country but also in England, and in 1837 his *General Observations on Vocal Music* was published in serial form in the *Musical World* (London).

So thorough was Mason, and so impressive were the results of his enterprise that, in due course, the School Board of Boston in 1838 went so far ahead of its time as to allocate public funds to the teaching of music. Unlike New York, which was much more inclined to rely on foreign musicians, Boston developed a strongly individual musical tradition, in which choral music, on all levels, took pride of place.

Much of the music composed for the children of Boston as a result of Lowell Mason's influence was of no great value. But some was fresh and delightful and well worth including in the present repertoire. Here, for example, is the chorus of one of the *Carols for Christmas, Easter, etc.*, composed by A. P. Howard and published in Boston in 1867 (Ex. 25).

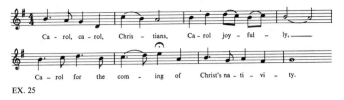

Ca - rol, ca - rol, Chris - tians, Ca - rol joy - ful - ly,——

Ca - rol for the com - ing of Christ's na - ti - vi - ty.

EX. 25

Meanwhile a new feature appeared on the musical-social landscape—the male-voice choir. The Glee Clubs of Britain, which had sponsored singing by small groups gradually gave way to larger bodies of men singers, for which a new repertoire was brought into being. The lead in establishing male-voice choirs, however, was taken by the Germans for whom the male-voice choral society became part of the new tradition of nationalism. Student bodies provided an informal background to this activity, but formality came with the institution of the *Liedertafel*. The term may be translated as "song-table" and was borrowed from the earlier *Tafelmusik* which was used to describe instrumental music for amateurs.

In 1809, Carl Friedrich Zelter became the President of the first *Liedertafel* to be founded, in Berlin. There were twenty-four members, divided into two groups of tenors and two groups of basses. "They assembled," according to the *Harmonicon* of 1833, "once a month, and sang their songs, the poetry and music being of their own production, their president making his remarks on them. In fact, it was a revival, in a much improved form, of the guild of the old German *Meistersänger*, and did no little credit to the state of cultivation, and the attainments of the dilettanti of Berlin."

The *Liedertafel* movement spread throughout Germany, both among the middle and the working classes. Societies bearing this name were also founded by German immigrants in England and in the United States. It was soon found impracticable for members of such groups to compose their own poetry and music. There was, therefore, a strong demand for new music.

Music was written by Carl Maria von Weber (1786–1826), Felix Mendelssohn, Robert Schumann (1810–56), Richard Wagner, as well as a large number of minor composers. Many of these songs, sentimental on the one hand, nationalist on the other, were of indifferent quality. This did not prevent them from becoming widely used, not only in Germany, but in other countries, where male-voice choirs were also popular. To this day most of the music sung by male-voice choirs, whether of university students in the United States or of miners in the valleys of Wales, is in the style of the *Liedertafel* songs of more than a hundred years ago.

The sentimental aspect of this style is demonstrated by an arrangement of *Die Lorelei*, a popular folk song well-known all over the world. In this example, taken from a collection published in Regensburg in 1866, it will be noticed that apart from the melody there is very little of interest for the singers. Germany gave the world some of its finest music, but it also produced some of the least good (Ex. 26).

EX. 26

What was true of one nation was also true of another. Nationalism was the greatest issue of the nineteenth century and in many European countries ideals of freedom and independence were promoted by means of song. In emulation of the Germans and Austrians many male-voice choirs were established in Northern, Central, and Eastern Europe. Thus it was that Pavel Krizkovsky (1820–85) arranged folk songs and composed part songs of a patriotic nature for the male-voice choirs of Czechoslovakia; that Leos Janacek (1854–1928), living in the industrial city of Brno, composed music that was both patriotic

[176]

and also an incentive to social action; that the great Hungarian composer, Ferenc Erkel (1810–93) led a great revival of choral singing in Hungary; that Mikhail Glinka (1803–57) and Peter Tchaikovsky (1840–93) wrote part songs and cantatas on Russian heroic subjects, composed church music for the Orthodox church, and arranged folk songs for choral use; and that Edvard Grieg (1843–1907) wrote Norwegian cantatas and made arrangements of Norwegian folk songs.

Taking everything into consideration, it is hardly surprising that the provision of choral music was high on the list of the nineteenth-century composer's list of priorities. In a period of great demand, quality is likely to be variable. Among the choral works—large and small—of the nineteenth century

[177]

there is a large quantity of bad music, an even larger quantity of what now seems indifferent music, and a handful of masterpieces.

Use of the term masterpieces needs some qualification, for in the field of vocal (especially choral) music a two-tier system operates. A masterpiece is a work which is accepted as such, without question, in many countries. At least half of the significance of a large-scale work for voices is in the words. If we do not know what the words are about, and if we cannot sing them with understanding, we find ourselves in great difficulties. When Latin was a commonly understood language, it was possible for a composer to wield influence through music for voices beyond his own country. To this day Latin remains a convenient medium. But in practice this restricts most of us to the traditional texts of the Mass, the Requiem Mass, and of a number of hymns—such as the *Stabat Mater*. In these the words have become familiar in one way or another. Apart from the convention that allows us to know the meaning of certain liturgical texts we are generally dependent on translations of texts from one language to another. In practice this has entailed translation from German into English, or English into German. Choral works in other languages have less frequently been transferred into either English or German, which means that being less than familiar they hardly qualify for consideration as musical masterpieces.

Handel had a long start and at least *Messiah* was translated into many languages. The two Haydn oratorios became widely known. The major works of Bach (the *B Minor Mass* and the *Magnificat*, of course, have Latin texts) crossed many frontiers. The one nineteenth-century oratorio that won undisputed and general popularity was Mendelssohn's *Elijah*.

Mendelssohn, himself of middle-class origin, was the ideal of the respectable middle classes in Germany and Britain during his lifetime, and for a long time afterwards. He was extremely clever, was an expert in public relations, had the ability to get on with people of influence, and was businesslike. His music was most graceful, charming, and balanced, and provoked no awkward questions for the listener to solve. In many instances, notably in movements or parts of movements that are now described as sentimental, Mendelssohn gave to his audiences what they wanted to hear. (To a greater or lesser degree most composers—often unconsciously—try to do this in so far as composition represents a relationship between composer and society.) In no case did Mendelssohn judge public taste better than in that of *Elijah*.

Mendelssohn's connections with England were close and he had enjoyed success with the oratorio *St. Paul* and the choral-symphonic *Hymn of Praise* at the Birmingham Festivals of 1837 and 1840. The first of these works had been composed for the Lower Rhine Musical Festival held at Düsseldorf in 1836; the second had its première in St. Thomas's Church, Leipzig in 1840. Both were also widely acclaimed in Germany. The composition of *Elijah* was the result of a direct commission from the Birmingham Musical Festival, and the first performance took place in Birmingham Town Hall on August 26, 1846, the composer conducting. Its success was overwhelming. In October, 1847, the first German performance of the work was given. A month later it was performed in the Tabernacle, New York, by the Sacred Music Society, conducted by T. Y. Chubb.

Apart from the wonderful, Bach-inspired overture, the strength of *Elijah* lies in its choral sonorities. These spring from a precise appreciation on the composer's part of what, in the way of spacing and dynamics, could be achieved by a large choral body. The choruses are dramatic not because of the skilful interplay of parts, as in Bach, but because of the effects of relatively simple contrasts of tone skilfully and dramatically placed. It should be added that the choral effects are brilliantly woven into the orchestral textures. *Elijah* is choral club music raised to a higher degree (just as the *St. Matthew Passion* is Kantorei music raised to a higher degree), and that was the principal reason for its enormous success in an age in which the choral society was at the heart of musical appreciation.

It should also be made clear that *Elijah* was attractive for other reasons. The London critic, H. F. Chorley, wrote after the first performance: "The world owes good thanks to Dr. Mendelssohn for having conformed his manner to his subject—for having treated the same religiously yet romantically."

The dramatic force of *Elijah* remained an abiding influence in choral music: the "religious and romantic" died away—though it was a long time in doing so.

The oratorio tradition, thus renewed by Mendelssohn, carried on, in accordance with the inclinations of choral society members with frequent roots in church choirs, throughout the nineteenth century. Sacred oratorios were produced in large numbers. Apart from *Elijah* almost the only survivors are *The Childhood of Christ*, finished by Hector Berlioz (1803–69) in 1854, and *The Dream of Gerontius* (Birmingham 1900) by Edward Elgar (1857–1934). The eternal attraction of the story of Christmas has been mentioned many times in this book. Berlioz treated this story with grace and charm in his oratorio, making no attempt to make it sound narrowly "religious". In view of modern techniques of placing groups of singers it is interesting to note that Berlioz gave precise instructions as to where his singers were to be situated during the performance of *The Childhood of Christ*. Elgar's *Dream of Gerontius*, the major oratorio by a native English composer, was a setting of an edited poem by Cardinal John Henry Newman. Like Berlioz, Elgar did not allow himself to be restricted by considerations of how "religious" music ought to sound. He used techniques that he had learned from many sources, particularly from Wagner. It may be said that both Berlioz and Elgar went ahead of their time. Both these works perplexed singers brought up in conventional ways; but both are firmly established in the modern repertoire.

By the side of the sacred oratorio, as it was called, there

also grew up a strong tradition of secular oratorio, or cantata. Many such works belonged to the nationalist movements of the times, and for that reason have tended to pass out of general appreciation. Each country has its own list of such works, which served a two-fold purpose. On the one hand they encouraged composers to compose, on the other they broadened the experience of the amateur music makers on whom the welfare of choral music, and music in general, depended. The illustration above shows the opening of the Philadelphia Exposition of 1876. The principal choral work for this occasion was the

[181]

Centennial Hymn by John Knowles Paine (1839–1906), one of the early notable composers of the United States, who had already achieved distinction by being the first American composer to conduct a work of his own, a setting of the Mass, at the famous Singakademie in Berlin.

Thus we see how the Mass retained its attraction for composers, even though not all of them were Catholic. The truth is, that the Mass is both lyrical and dramatic, and, apart from liturgical consideration, this fact is a permanent challenge to composers. Choral music, after all, is nothing if it is not either lyrical or dramatic; for this is the property of words which are the basis of choral composition.

With the *Missa Solemnis* of Beethoven, the Mass went from the confines of the church into the world. For better or worse this work became a concert piece, although its antecedents are inescapable. The two great successors to the Beethoven Mass, in that they appealed to the imagination of all music lovers, irrespective of their religious convictions, were the *Messe des Morts* (*Mass for the Dead* or *Requiem*) of Berlioz, and the *Requiem Mass* of Guiseppe Verdi (1813–1901).

It will now be noted that a fair proportion of choral music is dedicated to the subject of death. The reason is clear: this is one of the abiding themes that perplex the mind and stir the imagination of mankind. The great drama of death is seen by some as a kind of pageant, and so it was treated by the ritual of the Catholic church. Within the Requiems of Berlioz and Verdi, both brought up in Catholic environments, the sense of pageantry is present to a high degree.

Both works are of enormous scale, in every way monumental. Berlioz's Mass, performed in Paris in 1837, was in honour of French soldiers who had died in a campaign in Algeria (recently taken as a colony). Verdi's Requiem was a tribute to a great Italian patriot and writer, Alessandro Manzoni (1785–1873). It was performed for the first time in St. Mark's Church, Milan, in 1874. Berlioz was the great revolutionary composer of his age. His *Requiem* bears little resemblance to any familiar church music. Conceived for vast forces (with a choir of from 200–800 voices, and an orchestra proportionately large and augmented with separate and independent forces of brass instruments), it lies somewhere between the *Fantastic Symphony* (in which the ancient funeral hymn to be found in the service of the Requiem Mass—the *Dies Irae—Day of Wrath* —is parodied) and the vast operatic project of *The Trojans*. In all of these works, the theme of death appears, to be alternately welcomed and challenged by the vast, uneven, resources of Berlioz's imagination.

Verdi, one of the greatest opera composers of all time, makes his *Requiem* superbly operatic. For so long the theme of religious art, the subject is turned by Verdi into a marvellous sequence of rich and varied mural paintings in music. Much more than Berlioz's Mass does this conform to religious sentiment; but to Italian religious sentiment. The distinction between sacred and profane was always less marked in Catholic than in Protestant countries, despite what officials of the Church said from time to time.

One other Requiem of the nineteenth century retains a place in the choral repertoire: that is the *Deutsches Requiem* of Johannes Brahms (1833–97). This work was first performed in Bremen Cathedral in 1868.

In the liturgical sense, the *German Requiem* is not a Requiem at all, but a sequence of motets (with orchestral accompaniment) to texts, with death as their link, on words taken from Luther's Bible. Brahms, unlike Berlioz and Verdi, was experienced as a choral conductor and he had a high regard for the properties of choral music as maintained in the German tradition. In contrast to the Frenchman and the Italian, he employs vocal lines, finely placed in contrapuntal textures recalling Bach's procedures, rather than blocks of choral tone, to convey the musical argument. On the whole one can give a good impression of Brahms's *Requiem* (with piano accompaniment) with no

[183]

more than eight voices. This is not possible with Berlioz or Verdi. Brahms was economical rather than extravagant with his musical resources, cutting down rather than augmenting. This may, or may not, be a Protestant trait. Certainly the *German Requiem* is a very Protestant work, which has helped its popularity in Britain and America.

Although in every sense a work of its own day—as is evident in the harmonic and instrumental textures—the *German Requiem* suggests that the future of choral music is best guaranteed by reconsideration of the techniques of the past. In almost every movement we may feel the hidden influence of the German motets of the sixteenth and seventeenth centuries. The quality of the *German Requiem* is compassion. So we may hear the consoling voices of the opening movement (Ex. 27):

EX. 27

And we may compare with this the manner in which Heinrich Schütz once expressed himself. The link word is *Selig* (blessed). (Ex. 28).

EX. 28

II

Some New Trends

THE quotations given at the end of the last chapter, although separated in time by more than 200 years, show more in common than would excerpts from instrumental music of the same periods. Apart from the fact that both Schütz and Brahms were aware of the conventions within which choral music based on religious values was set, these examples illustrate the general limits within which it was thought choral singers should operate. The result of the acceptance of limitations led to the belief that the ideal end of choral music was to be expressed in terms of smooth, flowing parts for soprano, contralto, tenor and bass, with a strong preference for four-part harmonic textures.

Much music composed for choral societies at the end of the nineteenth and the beginning of the twentieth centuries was dull and unenterprising. As the choral society began to lose something of its social function (with the extension of recreational opportunities in other fields), its musical influence began to wane. A generation ago, choir members were able, by packing an auditorium with relatives and friends, to make a choral performance very much a family affair. This is no longer the case. The public that once automatically assembled to listen to *Messiah* or *Elijah*, or, (to take a work which, now almost entirely ignored, once enjoyed great popularity) *Hiawatha*, by Samuel Coleridge-Taylor (1875–1912), has almost disappeared. An exception may be made, however, for performances by school choirs, which still attract automatic good will and family patronage.

In general the musical public as a whole show a clear preference for orchestral music. Choral items in the standard symphony concert repertoire are rare, except where voices form an integral part of the symphonic texture. The composition of "choral symphonies" has attracted many composers if for no other reason than that words can be used to throw light on ideas that lie at the root of some instrumental music. A climactic work in the tradition of choral symphony is the eighth symphony of Gustav Mahler (1860–1911).

This symphony, however, is nearer to the oratorio than to the symphonic tradition. Originally planned with outer choral movements enclosing two purely instrumental sections, it was reduced to two parts; the first part being a setting of the ancient hymn *Veni Creator spiritus* (*Come, Holy Ghost*), the second part a setting of the end score of Goethe's *Faust* (Part II). Mahler employed boys' chorus, mixed-voice chorus, and an enormously expanded orchestra for this work. It was first performed in a hall specially built for the purpose, in Munich, in the autumn of 1910—three years after the work had been completed.

At that point in the history of music, the cultivation of size for its own sake was on the wane. Mahler's eighth symphony, mockingly known as the "symphony of a thousand", was greeted unenthusiastically by German and Austrian critics. Of late years Mahler has enjoyed much popularity in the United States and Britain, and a performance of the eighth symphony was given in 1964 in the cathedral in Liverpool. The forces then used may be regarded as the minimum: they were 520 singers, and 180 orchestral musicians. Clearly, this kind of music requires intensive joint rehearsal of singers and players. It is equally clear that under present economic conditions it is not easy to arrange the necessary rehearsals.

This fact alone tends to operate against extensive large-scale choral-orchestral activity. Not so long ago amateur choirs rehearsed standard oratorios (and cantatas) to piano accompaniment, and joined up with the orchestra, perhaps once (sometimes not at all!) before a public performance. At the present time, the gap between all but a few choirs of amateur singers and highly professional orchestras is considerable: and the contemporary audience goes for virtuosity.

So far as choral music performance of virtuoso quality is concerned this is looked for either from the substantial choruses maintained by some broadcasting companies; by special bodies such as the New Philharmonia Choir in London of which the members are professional; by choirs with long traditions maintained by religious foundations, such as those in Vienna, Cambridge, and Leipzig; by spectacular bodies to which a certain exotic quality is attached—as, for instance, the Red Army Choir; by highly trained school choirs, such as those made famous in Budapest through association with the music of Kodály and Bartók, or that of Princeton High School which has successfully toured in Europe, or by small and select choral groups, which frequently concentrate their attention on particular types of music. Dr. Alfred Mann, of Rutgers University, New Jersey, has done much to promote high standards of Handel interpretation and, as writer and editor, exerted a beneficial influence on choral music in general. The next illustration shows the Rutgers University Choir, with Dr. Mann conducting. Throughout the world there are similar choirs which make a speciality of medieval music, or of madrigals, or of Bach, or of modern works.

This suggests, what is true, that the former unity of choral music has been split. No longer does one think in terms of, as the catalogues put it, S.A.T.B.

None the less, what may be termed the main-stream choral-society tradition has been maintained. This is due to the vitality of festivals, in which choral music plays a large part, to the need for works for special celebrations, and to the attraction of composers to the choral-orchestral medium. Relatively few of such

[187]

works have established themselves as undisputed classics, for which the reason is not necessarily any inferiority within the music but rather to lack of opportunity, already explained, to make large-scale choral works widely known.

Of the main-stream works—that is, those which appear to follow naturally on the stylistic developments and practices of the nineteenth century—these are widely known: *The Hymn of Jesus*, by Gustav Holst (1874–1934), the *Psalmus Hungaricus*, by Zoltán Kodály (1882–1967), *Belshazzar's Feast*, by William Walton (b. 1902), *Carmina burana* by Carl Orff (b. 1895), and the *War Requiem* by Benjamin Britten (b. 1913).

Walton's work, composed for the Leeds Festival, exciting on account of its sonorities, its rhythmic energy, and its power of description, is, perhaps, the most conventional of these works. The manner in which the composer emphasized the dramatic qualities of the text, however, disturbed those who in 1931 considered that choral music should be entirely respectable—a kind of branch line from approved church music. But if we listen carefully to many of Handel's oratorio choruses we may well feel that Walton was only doing in the twentieth century what Handel and Bach were doing in the eighteenth.

Composed some fifteen years before Walton's oratorio, *The Hymn of Jesus* has this in common with it: a vivid rhythmic structure which is often distinguished by 5/4 or 7/4 time. The words of this work are from apocryphal, middle-eastern sources, and strongly mystical. The mysticism is reflected in the frequently unusual harmonic procedures of Holst (based to some extent on Tudor principles), in the use of a semi-chorus placed away from the main body of singers, in unusual vocal effects (see p. 195), in the orchestration and in the use of plainsong *motive*, which are set out, in free rhythm, in the Prelude.

Strongly-marked rhythms make a distinctive feature of twentieth-century music, and choral singers brought up on the conventions of nineteenth-century practice have needed to adjust themselves to a higher degree of dynamism in performance.

[189]

Carl Orff's *Carmina burana*, heavily and percussively orchestrated, is almost brutal in its rhythmic urgency, and this aspect of the work is emphasized by a great simplicity of harmony. Remembering practices to be found in so-called primitive music (a constant source of inspiration to Orff), the composer makes great use of the basic intervals of fundamental harmony. *Carmina burana* (which was designed for stage presentation) was based on ribald poems from the thirteenth century, taken from a manuscript in a Bavarian monastery, and was first performed in Frankfurt in 1937.

These works testify to the greater importance placed on the literary values of text in the twentieth century, and also to a general tendency to renew choral techniques by reconsidering the fundamentals of the choral tradition, with particular reference to the Middle Ages.

Kodály's *Psalmus Hungaricus*, like Britten's *War Requiem*, was a piece for an occasion. It was composed in 1923 to celebrate the Jubilee of the federation of the two cities that make Budapest. Taking a poignant seventeenth-century Hungarian poem and by setting it in the style that he evolved from Hungarian folk song Kodály made a great impression with this work, which now has the status almost of a national hymn. Composed for the opening of the new cathedral in Coventry and first performed in 1962, Britten's *War Requiem* combines the words of the Latin Requiem Mass with a series of moving poems by Wilfrid Owen (1893–1918). The theme of this work —abhorrence of war—caught the ear of the world, and it is doubtful whether any other choral work has, within a year or two of its composition, made such a dramatic impact. This is partly due to the character of the text, but it is also due to Britten's genius in expressing his thoughts in an idiom which, while original, raises no barriers of technique before the listener. There are, however, many problems for the performers. Like many modern choral works the *War Requiem* depends on the exploitation of space, and the placing of groups

[190]

of singers and instrumentalists at different points in a large building.

Of the composers named, all, except Walton, have exercised a strong and beneficial influence on amateur music making and music in education in general, and on choral music in particular. There are many fine pieces, especially by Holst, Kodály, and Britten, for different combinations of voices, and of voices and instruments, which achieve their aims without letting go of the principles that have ruled choral music for the past three centuries.

The present age is one of revolution, or, rather, of a series of revolutions. In such an age, there is inevitably an overlap of traditions. Just as in the seventeenth century the traditional style of the polyphonic composers ran over the new monodic style, so today we find much music being composed that, broadly speaking, could have been composed a generation ago. Music which is termed conservative is more frequently to be found in the general choral repertoire, simply because the bulk of amateur choral singers (who often live away from main centres of musical activity), are conservative so far as music is concerned. (To be fair, judging by the popularity ratings of orchestral works in concert programmes or recording lists, choral singers are no more conservative than the general body of music lovers.) This is a fact, neither to be deplored nor applauded but simply to be taken into account. At the same time (and this is not really new) there are amateur choral bodies that are enterprising, anxious to involve themselves in the new music of the twentieth century. Not surprisingly these are to be found in universities, other institutes of higher education, and schools throughout the world.

Choral music, more than any other form of music, can reflect revolutionary ideas, can in itself be revolutionary, or by combining ideas and techniques—which is what composers attempt to do anyway—can do both at the same time. The words of a choral work, which are the starting point, may very well illustrate new lines of thought in religion, politics or social affairs in general. It sometimes happens that composers choose texts of a provocative nature, but then rob them of significance by setting them to music that is less than challenging. Sometimes techniques become an end in themselves and detract from the meaning of the texts. The ideal work is one in which ideas stated in words are matched by music that puts no barrier between the two forms of expression, nor between the work and the listener.

The general aim of the modern composer is to release music from the idea of "art for art's sake". This principle, when it was practised, gave to music, as well as other forms of artistic expression, a particular kind of unreality. This was evident in many, now-forgotten, nineteenth-century oratorios, anthems, Masses and so on. Music for the church was judged not by its liturgical effectiveness, nor by its expression of the basic values contained in the words, but by the pleasure it appeared to give, and a capacity not to offend.

Many composers, conscious of this distortion of values, have made strenuous attempts to bring liturgical music, or music on religious themes, back to fundamental principles. Two works in particular, twentieth-century classics, stand out in this respect; the *Symphony of Psalms* (1930) and the *Mass* (1948) of Igor Stravinsky (b. 1882). The former was composed in commemoration of the Jubilee of the Boston Symphony Orchestra, the latter was intended solely for liturgical use. The *Symphony of Psalms* is a remarkable combination of choral principles with symphonic procedures. It is in three contrasted movements (the words of which come from different Psalms): a prelude, a double fugue, and an exuberant finale. These three movements make a musical unity, which supports the unity of faith given by a prayer for divine pity, a recognition of divine grace, and a hymn of praise. The vocal unity is taut, direct, strongly contrapuntal. The orchestra adds to the directness of the expression by omitting the more or less emotional qualities of violins and violas.

The *Mass* (in which solo voices alternate with chorus) is even
more taut, and the structure of the music, supported by double
wind quintet, near to the practices of late fifteenth-century
Flemish composers. Both works are remarkable for their intensity of thought, their serious intention, and their sincerity.
The brief passage quoted below shows the economy of the
style, the flexibility of the rhythms, and the direct, often dis-
cordant, character of the counterpoint. Note the effectiveness
of the strongest discord to underline the word *peccata* (*sins*).
Within the last twenty years Stravinsky has written other choral
works, which have increasingly reflected his absorption within
the musical problems of our time, and of which the ultimate
standing remains to be judged (Ex. 29).

EX. 29

Religious music, in that it starts from the premise that it can
influence the way in which people think, is, to use a modern
term, ideological. But Christianity now appears as one among
a number of ideologies. In contrast to the principles of
Christianity are those which grew from the philosophy of Karl
Marx and from the revolutionary ideals that followed on

[193]

Marx's teaching. The working-class movement of the nineteenth century found artistic expression through choral societies. In the twentieth century the protest of the working classes against exploitation by capitalism, and degradation through mass unemployment, as well as protest against other forms of tyranny inspired the choral works of Hanns Eisler (1898–1962), an idealistic and courageous German composer whose opinions made it necessary for him to go into exile during the 1930s. Eisler, a pupil of Schoenberg in Vienna, and a friend of the dramatist Berthold Brecht, evolved a highly personal style distinguished by its simplicity, but also by its toughness and its sincerity. Eisler's music is that of a man concerned about human beings, and it sounds like it.

The spread of Communism has led to a new kind of orthodoxy in countries where the system is strong. This orthodoxy is to be appreciated in numerous choral works which, based on simple and conservative techniques intended to win the attention of the uneducated, are not often of outstanding interest. A characteristic work of this kind is *A Day of my country* (1953) by Alexei Machavariani (b. 1913), a leading composer of Georgia, in the U.S.S.R. Scored for soloists, children's and adult choruses, and orchestra, partly based on Georgian folk song, this secular oratorio gives "vivid musical pictures of life in Georgia and glorifies its people". Of works of this kind, partly ideological but continuing the nationalist traditions of the nineteenth century, there is a large number.

War and peace; oppression and freedom: these lie deep in the texture of much choral music the world over. The *War Requiem* of Britten has a parallel in the *Requiem for those who died in the war against fascism* (1963) by Dmitri Kabalevsky (b. 1904), in which children's voices are used in addition to mixed voice choir to express the idea of hope in the future.

The passion which inspires contemporary idealism comes less from dogmatic sources, however, than from a belief in the significance of man. Although this is not precisely formulated

—nor, perhaps, is it possible to do so, even though attempts have been made—it amounts to a belief in humanism. More than ever before artists (with their own values under assault from many sides) have become involved in the burning questions of the day. There are many choral works, other than those already named, to testify to this.

Arnold Schoenberg (1874–1951), one of the architects of contemporary music, whose oratorio *Jacob's Ladder* and opera *Moses and Aaron* belong to the tradition of sacred music-drama although their techniques are far away from traditional techniques, wrote the moving cantata *A Survivor from Warsaw* (for speaker, men's chorus and orchestra), shortly after the Second World War. The French composer Francis Poulenc (1899–1963), inspired by the Resistance Movement during the war composed a moving cantata, of which the theme is belief in the eventual triumph of liberty. This was *Figure humaine* (*The Face of Man*), and was based on poems by Paul Eluard. The music of Stravinsky and Schoenberg is often intellectually demanding; that of Poulenc asks less in this respect, for his style is lyrical and intentionally simple.

Style is less important than what a composer does with it. In our day there is not, as there was in the eighteenth century, a general style of which the main principles are generally observed. There are almost as many styles as there are composers. The range from Schoenberg to Poulenc is wide, and between these two poles of stylistic expression there is a wealth of individual examples. On the whole, the tendency is towards freedom of expression. That the virtual destruction of tonal system has led to other precepts which are sometimes accepted too readily does not cancel out the fact that composers of stature treat each individual work as a separate problem, to be solved by examination of the sonorities and structures possible for and proper to the particular case.

In the *Hymn of Jesus* Holst made effective use of choral speech, and the way in which the various parts of the chorus follow each other in a contrapuntal texture of voices at in-determinate pitch with the words "Glory to thee . . ." is im-pressive. So too is the manner in which the composer gives an idea of the endlessness of wisdom by making the chorus close their tone to a humming tone, through closed lips, on the final consonant. Since that time the territory that joins speech to music has been more fully exploited. The use of a speaking voice against an orchestral and sometimes choral texture is not par-ticularly new, for it was tried out in "melodramatic" music of the romantic era. A good example is Schumann's treatment of a long poem by Byron in *Manfred*—a work that has been effec-tively revived in recent years. It is, of course, easy to set speech in contrast to singing. It is more difficult to bring the two into harmony with one another. That is what contemporary com-posers often try to do.

Of pre-war works one of the most interesting was the oratorio *The Fall of Wagadu through Pride*, by the German–Russian composer, Vladimir Vogel (b. 1896). Driven out of Germany by the events of the times, Vogel settled in Switzerland. *The Fall of Wagadu* was based on an African legend (dealing with the destruction of the kingdom of Wagadu through pride, treachery, greed, and internal strife). It was first performed in Brussels in 1935. During the war all the scores and parts were destroyed, but the composer rewrote the whole work from memory and it was revived in 1955. In this oratorio the chorus plays the leading role and is allotted both speaking and singing parts. Soloists, including solo speakers, are drawn from the chorus. In planning his instrumentation, Vogel aimed at sounds that, in his view, come closest to the human voice. So the work is scored for five saxophones and clarinet.

The relation of indeterminate to determinate vocal values, and of both to instrumental sonorities was thoroughly explored by the British composer (of Spanish origin), Roberto Gerhard (b. 1896), in a large-scale choral-orchestral work inspired by, and based on, Albert Camus's novel *The Plague*. This book dealt

[196]

with an imaginary outbreak of plague, and its consequences, in the North African town of Oran some twenty years ago. A symbolic work, the aim of the novel was to awaken the conscience of people to a general responsibility for particular catastrophes. There was a time when disasters were put down as acts of divine displeasure. In the twentieth century most disaster are man-made, and, in theory, avoidable.

Gerhard was deeply influenced by this novel and *The Plague*, an alternation of chorus pieces and spoken narrative is a fine musical tract for the times. On the technical side, Gerhard avoided solo singers, in order not to over-dramatize the text and in order that the personality of the composer should not appear to intrude. For the same reason there are no orchestral interludes. The whole of the music is regarded as a fabric of sounds, with the spoken parts as valid as those that are sung. Besides singing, the chorus whispers, speaks and shouts, while the narrator's voice, kept on an unemotional level, is one sound pattern among others. Nor is this all. The indeterminacy of some instrumental sounds, as of percussion, the stringed instruments and the strings of the piano, is exploited to create a meeting point for instrumental and vocal sonorities.

This meeting point has been a point of departure for many younger composers, among them the Polish musician Krzystof Penderecki (b. 1933), whose *Passion according to St. Luke* is one of the most remarkable choral works of the 1960s. This work, which was first performed in Münster, Germany, is a comprehensive essay in contemporary techniques. The chorus is required to whisper, and to murmur, as well as to sing. Planned for three choirs, each of sixteen voices, Penderecki borrowed the polychoral (many choir) method from the Italian composers of the late Renaissance period. The thematic construction ranges from the idiom of Gregorian melody to the so-called twelve-note method developed by Schoenberg out of atonalism. In short, Penderecki's work is a bringing together

[197]

of different styles out of which one fresh and individual style apt to the particular work is created.

To perform such music, a virtuoso choir is needed. Is the day of the amateur choral singer then ended?

The answer, fortunately, is no. For with the new freedom accorded to the composer there comes also a new discipline: to shape each work according to the resources available. The day when oratorio or cantata implied a standardized body of singers is long past, and while mixed-voice choruses have an enormous repertoire on which to draw the future seems to lie with less standardized forces. This is particularly the case in school music, where the resources of one school vary greatly from those of another. At the top, there is the ordered excellence of the High School Choir; at the bottom is the disordered charm of the primary class. The resourceful modern composer takes the lot into consideration, adjusting the means to the ends.

Choral music certainly continues to fulfil all its ancient functions. There are, however, new functions, and in their performance the human values of music are maintained. New choral music, with vocal lines which include intervals that were once thought unvocal, with complex and frequently exciting rhythms, with vivid and stimulating texts, challenges the choral singer. But that is as it should be. It was at such a point that the broad choral tradition began, when the music of the church was transferred to secular use, when the motet style crossed over into that of the madrigal. On the whole, if you go back to Thomas Morley, on p. 96, and follow his advice, you can go on from there. The world of choral music is wide.

[198]

Glossary of Foreign Words

Movements of the Service of the Mass; these terms are used by the Roman Catholic Church, of which the liturgy is in Latin (although it is now permitted to use the vernacular). The expressions given below are sometimes used in English and American Episcopalian churches, and also (particularly the first two) in the Lutheran Church.

Greek   Kyrie [eleison]—Lord [have mercy]
Latin   Gloria [in excelsis]—Glory [in the highest]
  „   Credo—I believe [in God]
  „   Sanctus—Holy, [holy, holy]
  „   Agnus Dei—Lamb of God

Works and Recordings

This is a very small selection of available recordings, but they represent works which are important in appreciating the wide range of choral music.

Chapter 2

John Dunstable, Sacred and Secular Music, EA 36; Turn. (3) 4058
Guillaume Dufay, Mass *L'homme armé*, LYR. (7) 150

Chapter 3

Jacob Obrecht, Mass *Sub tuum praesidium*, DGG, ARC–198406
Orlandus Lassus, *St. Matthew Passion*, Dover 5268/7268
Pierluigi da Palestrina, *Stabat Mater*, Argo (5) 398
Giovanni Francesco Anerio, *Requiem Mass*, Oiseau 50211/60042

Chapter 4

Heinrich Isaac, Motets, Count. 5546
Heinrich Schütz, Psalms, None. 71134

Chapter 5

Thomas Morley, Ballets and Madrigals (with John Wilbye), Van. S–157
Thomas Weelkes, Madrigals, 3–West. (S) 1006

Chapter 6

Claudio Monteverdi, *Vespers*, 2–Van. C–10001/2
Henry Purcell, *Te Deum*, Ang. 5–36528

Chapter 7

Georg Frideric Handel, *Messiah*, 3–Phi. PHS–3–992
   Coronation Anthems, Argo (5) 369
Dietrich Buxtehude, *Missa Brevis, Magnificat*, Urania (5) 8018
Johann Sebastian Bach, *St. Matthew Passion*, 4–West. WST–402
   Mass in B minor, 3–Ang. 3500

Chapter 8

William Billings, Hymns and Anthems, Col. ML–5496/MS–6161
Josef Haydn, *St. Nicholas Mass*, Phi. 900134
Wolfgang Amadeus Mozart, *Requiem Mass*, Pick. S–4039

Chapter 9

Josef Haydn, *The Creation*, 2–Turn. 34184/5

Chapter 10

Ludwig van Beethoven, *Mass in D*, 2–Van. S–214/5
Felix Mendelssohn, *Elijah*, 3–Ang. 3558
Hector Berlioz, *L'Enfance du Christ*, 2–Vox SVUX–52009
Edward Elgar, *The Dream of Gerontius*, 2–Ang. S–3660
Johannes Brahms, *German Requiem*, 2–Ang. S–3624

Chapter 11

Zoltán Kodály, *Psalmus Hungaricus*, Mer. 90467
Carl Orff, *Carmina burana*, Cap. (S) PAR–8470
Benjamin Britten, *War Requiem*, 2–Lon. 1255
Igor Stravinsky, *Symphony of Psalms*, Vic. LSC–2822
　　　　　　　　 Mass (1948), Col. ML–6391/MS–6991
Krzystof Penderecki, *Passion according to St. Luke*, 2–Vic. VIC (S)–6015

Index